DIVE, DIVE!

Stan Smith

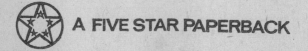

A FIVE STAR PAPERBACK

Dedicated to shipmates
who stayed out there . . .

This edition published in MCMLXXII by
PBS Limited, Victoria Mills, Pollard Street,
Manchester M4 7AU

Made and printed in Great Britain by
C. Nicholls & Company Ltd
The Philips Park Press, Manchester

DIVE, DIVE!

Author's Note

This anthology is primarily concerned with the actions of submariners under a given set of circumstances, usually adverse, but not necessarily so. Having been a submariner myself, and having written extensively on the subject, the compilation of this work was for me a labor of love. But it was more than that. It was attempting to tell a story, in several parts, of a unique service that carried the war to the enemy's doorstep.

Much of the material came directly from the Naval Archives and my friend, Mr. Dean Allard. Other material came from many of the personalities found herein who contributed their own epochal submarine incidents.

These stories are of American submarines in action during World War II. One section—*Into Action*—was added to the original material to bring the reader through the earliest phase of the conflict. Otherwise, nothing special has been added except perhaps a dash of enthusiasm for the project by my editor, Mrs. Gail Wendroff, and myself.

Bibliography included Rear Admiral Samuel Eliot Morison's History of the *U.S. Naval Operations in World War II*, and Theodore Roscoe's *Submarine*.

Stan Smith
Orleans, Mass.

THE DAY THE DEAD CAME BACK

No account of submarines would be complete without mention of Squalus, *resurrected from the dead in May of 1940, after 113 days of salvage operations and later rechristened* Sailfish. *"Squailfish" as the cognoscenti called her, chalked up an enviable record in the unremitting submarine war against Japan by sinking forty-five thousand tons of high priority shipping. Under Lieutenant Commander R. E. M. Ward (presently Rear Admiral)* Sailfish *performed the herculean feat of sinking the escort carrier* Chuyo *during a typhoon. This story, an account of the day twenty-six men died aboard her off the New England coast, will serve well to point up the thin line of demarcation between life and death in a submarine.*

At 7:30 A.M., May 23, 1939, Lieutenant Oliver F. Naquin stood on the bridge of the *Squalus,* conning the new 1,450-tonner down Maine's Piscatauqua River, on her way to sea and fleet test dives. It was clear and bright; river slightly choppy. As the submarine churned past the harbor entrance and veered on a course beyond Whaleback Reef, Naquin relinquished the deck to his OOD, Lieutenant William T. Doyle.

7

"She's all yours, Bill. Give me a call when we're nearly on station."

Doyle nodded and the skipper swiveled around, ducking into the conning tower hatch. Forward, gathered in the wardroom over coffee and cigarettes, were the three civilian observers from the Portsmouth Navy Yard, where *Squalus* had been built. They and Naquin discussed the day's program: a sixteen knot surface speed on four mains and then, with the diving alarm, full submergence within sixty seconds. These were routine requirements for any submarine about to join the fleet.

So far, all was normal.

On the bridge, Bill Doyle was coming up on his ranges and notifying the control room that the submarine was almost in her precise diving area. Then Naquin went topside to resume command of his bridge. It was 8:30 A.M.

"Rig for diving!" came the order. The Yard men climbed to the bridge and stood with their stopwatches in hand. Speed: sixteen knots.

"All right, pull the plug," the skipper said evenly. Doyle immediately hit the diving alarm twice. Below, a voice sounded over the intercom in raucous signal: "Dive! Dive!"

Time: 8:39 A.M.

In the moments before the disaster struck, Radioman 1/c Arthur L. Booth tapped out the routine diving message to the Navy Yard, notifying Rear Admiral Cyrus W. Cole that one of his pig boats was going under.

At her conning tower, draped around the handles of her periscope, was Lieutenant [jg] Bob Robertson. Naquin had left to join the Yard people, and stopwatch in hand, he checked the rate of descent. At periscope depth, procedure called for a leveling off and a check of all compartments.

Squalus was now dipping under the fifty foot mark, trimming herself. One of the Yard representa-

Ship's Cook William Isaacs was clawing his way toward the door.

Maness and company defied orders for a moment as the ashen-faced sailor, last to come forward, struggled toward them. Isaacs, within arm's reach of the trio, was jerked bodily through the watertight door to life.

In the control area all was silent as the submarine suddenly slid down to 240 feet, her bow tilted slightly at an eleven degree rise angle. Naquin, forcing a cool command despite the horror about him, swiveled around to Gunner's Mate E. Don Cravens and snapped:

"Red smoke bomb—fire it now!"

In the forward torpedo room was Lieutenant John Nichols. Naquin now ordered his Talker to pass the word for Nichols to release the forward marker buoy. Communication between these compartments was still extant, and this, in itself, was something, for aft all now was deadly silent. Here, in the control room, crewmen grimly adjusted themselves to the water-high combination of fuel oil and sea water, hanging on to whatever they could, gritting against the fear that nagged at their guts.

Meanwhile, in the Portsmouth Navy Yard, 11:30 A.M. had rolled around without a surfacing signal from Lieutenant Oliver Naquin's Squalus. At 11:45 A.M. Rear Admiral Cole, anxious for some kind of report, told Portsmouth Radio to send out her call sign and try to raise her. Nothing came back by way of a signal. Cole, an alert and conscientious submarine officer, was worried. He notified the Coast Guard, which reported that there were no subs operating in Squalus' assigned area. Remembering that another new sub—the Sculpin—had been due to take off for Panama at about eleven-thirty, Cole rushed down to the Portsmouth docks, desperately hoping that she'd been delayed.

Fortunately, she had. Cole reached the docks and

tives, smiling broadly as he watched the hand of his stopwatch lose the race, turned to Naquin.

"Nice goin', Captain. Looks like your lady's in—"

At that moment, Yeoman 1/c Charles S. Kuney, the compartments Talker, swiveled around to Naquin:

"Sir!" he blurted. *"The engine rooms are flooding!"*

"Take her up!" Naquin roared. In an instant, the exec barked the orders to blow all main ballast, safety, bow buoyancy—and to close watertight doors and flappers. *"For Christ's sake, take her up!"*.

Squalus dipped her bow sharply. But as high pressure air roared into the ballast tanks, the boat leveled off for a few moments at seventy feet. In the control room and conning tower, grim-faced sailors raced through the motions of saving the submarine. But, quivering in its death throes, *Squalus* slipped downward, her power lost, and settled to the bottom with her bow pointed sharply at a forty degree angle.

The rumble of water pouring into the after spaces filled the ears of Naquin's frenzied men. Galvanized into action by these first terrible seconds of looming eternity, submariners were quick to act: Electrician's Mate 3/c Lloyd Maness, in the after battery compartment, sloshed against the steep up angle trying to reach the bulkhead door aft. His orders were to put it on dog, no matter who was locked out in the after spaces.

Desperately straining to reach the bulkhead, the electrician found two shipmates at his side—Radioman 1/c Arthur Booth and Electrician 3/c John Batick—and now the trio of sweating, half-drowned sailors fumbled with the dogs. From the crew's quarters aft shouts of panic rose from the men trapped in the rising cataclysm of sea. Maness, leading this party, heard Naquin's sharply bawled command, *"Close watertight doors!"* but hesitated for a moment.

hailed *Sculpin's* skipper, Lieutenant Commander Warren D. Wilkin.

"Get underway!" the admiral snapped. "I want you to make a thorough search of the area. Something must have happened to Naquin's boat!"

Sculpin cast off.

Cole hurried back to his office. There, picking up a phone, he ordered tug *Penacock* to stand by for orders. Next, he contacted New London, asking the base skipper to have submarine rescue vessel *Falcon* standing by.

In the control room of Lieutenant Oliver Naquin's submarine, the air was getting heavy and foul. Forward, in the torpedo room, this condition already existed. Now Naquin gave the word to spread soda lime on available flat surfaces; also to bleed oxygen into the compartments from the boat's dwindling supply. There were a few emergency rations, some crackers in the officer's mess, but nothing more.

"We conserve everything," Naquin said tightly. "It may be a long wait before anybody comes out, so don't think about eating and don't move around much."

In the forward room, Nichols was saying essentially the same thing. If rescue came at all, and there was no indication that it would at this stage, the Rescue Chamber would be lowered from a submarine vessel and clamped securely in place on the trunk hatch on the forward room. There were two trunks, one aft in the now silent torpedo room and one forward in a corresponding position forward. At these depths, the Momsen Lung which required a "free" ascent along a marked line, was useless.

Everything depended upon someone spotting the smoke bombs.

On the surface of the Atlantic, submarine *Sculpin's* bridge was crowded with officers and sailors peering at the water with the intensity that marked their mission. Other than stray timber and a lobster pot,

nothing had been seen on the bland and now calm
surface of the ocean. But the bridge crew, mindful
of what was riding on a sighting, combed the water
with uncommon thoroughness. Then:

"Sir, red smoke rocket off the port bow! Range one
mile!"

Sculpin veered on course and zeroed in on the puff
of red smoke. Range closed inexorably in a rush
of white water. Then Wilkin gave the order that
slowed her to a crawl as a lookout, moments later,
bawled the marker was five hundred yards ahead.
The submarine stopped parallel to the buoy and a
crewman grappled it aboard. Inside, Wilkin's eager
hands found the telephone he knew would be there
He pressed his lips into the phone.

"Below! On the *Squalus*—can you read me?"

In the forward torpedo room of the trapped submarine, startled men heard the sudden squawk from
above. Jubilantly, Oliver Naquin abandoned control
and fought his way forward. But at this critical moment Fate intervened and the phone went dead.
Lieutenant Nichols repeated the message from
above.

"Thank God!" Naquin mumbled softly. "Thank
God!"

He wheeled around to the men in the forward
torpedo room.

"Break out hammers and mauls. You men who can
read Morse code, start tapping. I'm going back to
control to do the same there!"

Topside, Warren Wilkin was sending off his good
news to Admiral Cole at the Portsmouth Navy Yard.

Shortly after 10 P.M., May 24, the tug *Penacock*
reached the scene with rescue vessel *Falcon* running
a close second. Chief Boatswain's Mate Martin
Sibitzky, master diver, was sitting on the deck fully
garbed for the underwater journey.

Sibitzky and the rescue chamber [eighteen thousand pounds] went over at the same time, a long

excruciating booming procedure of which the men trapped in the *Squalus* were oblivious. There had been no sounds from above except the faintly audible sound of many thrashing propellers, but nothing more. Even the tapping had stopped.

Time: 11:40 A.M.; more than twenty-six hours after Wilkin's sub had spotted the smoke bomb, the rescue of *Squalus* commenced.

In *Squalus*, the men in the forward torpedo room and control room waited tensely for the rescue they knew was at hand. Few had more than shut their eyes since that first horrible moment of tragedy, for scuttlebutt had it that if a man dropped into a deep sleep, the chances were that he'd never wake up again. The air was heavy and the food had given out. Bleary-eyed, shivering sailors huddled in the near-darkness of red-glowing battle lamps, watching the overhead.

Meanwhile, in the bell-shaped chamber, along with Martin Sibitzky, were Torpedoman 1/c John Mikalowski and Gunner's Mate 1/c Walter E. Harmon. With Sibitzky's guidance, the bell was fitted onto the torpedo escape hatch and a signal tapped to the two sailors inside. Then the diver went up to report to an anxious Admiral Cole that the rescue chamber was now fitted to *Squalus'* deck.

In the chamber, the two sweating specialists quickly brought their wrenches into play. The gasketed bottom of the compartment was now fitted to the escape trunk of the submarine and, at a signal to *Falcon,* a supply of air blew the bell dry. Mikalowski slithered down into the blown section, attaching toggle bars and pad-eyes on the sub's hatch access. Now the torpedoman climbed into the chamber and tapped with his stilson wrench on the cover of the sub. Incredulous submariners heard the scraping of metal against metal—then the hatch cover bent inward! Mikalowski shouted down into the chorus of wild shouts.

Hands reached eagerly to pump the hand of life, and then the torpedoman passed into the submarine hot coffee and smokes, after which the forward room was given a jolt of fresh air from the Rescue Chamber. In control, too, wildly cheering men knew the full story now. Mikalowski's work was half done. Nine of the crew in the worst condition came aboard he rescue chamber first, later nine more—and finally Naquin's crew from the control room.

In all, thirty-three survivors!

On the *Falcon,* Rear Admiral Cole—exhausted as if he himself had been below—gave Lieutenant Commander Floyd Tusler orders to begin the recovery of the doomed submarine.

Exactly 113 days later, through the use of pontoons, the recovery was accomplished and *Squalus* came up from the depths. Taken to the Portsmouth Navy Yard where twenty-six dead men were removed, the submarine was placed out of commission.

But in May 1940 *Squalus* was recommissioned into the United States Navy and given a new name—*Sailfish.* She went on to sink seven Jap ships in World War II.

Ironically, *Sculpin,* the submarine which spotted the smoke bomb, died in the waters of the Marianas, victim of a crack enemy antisubmarine escort vessel.

Squalus, whom she had retrieved from the dead, came back . . . .

INTO ACTION

SEVEN DAYS after Vice Admiral Chuichi Nagumo's Pearl Harbor striking force sent the United States Pacific Fleet battleships to the bottom, an American submarine fired torpedoes at a Japanese merchant ship.

Unhappily the target was only damaged. But this American gesture of defiance clearly presaged events to come.

The first enemy merchant ship died only a few days later—December 15, 1941—when Lieutenant Commander Chester C. Smith conned *Swordfish* into a decisive night attack off Hainan Island. Four fish streaked down the track "straight, hot and true," and down went the 8,700 ton *Atsutusan Maru*.

There were other blazing actions during the frantic weeks immediately following the Pearl Harbor debacle, but it wasn't until January 27 that the Imperial Japanese Navy suffered its maiden fatality of the Pacific campaign. These were the circumstances attending the explosive demise of I-173; 1,785 tons.

Midway Island, soon to be the highly desired objective of a major IJN thrust, was under close surveillance by Admiral Yamamoto's submarines. Three of these were under way that day to look things over and, in the process, lob a few 5-inch shells at the island's defenders. Twenty-four hours, before Lieutenant Commander Elton H. Grenfell's *Gudgeon* received an intercept from Comsubpac: one of the I-class submarines was heading his way!

Already on a long, unproductive war patrol in the immediate area, Grenfell (presently Vice Admiral) simply altered course to converge and, within a few hours, his doughty command was positioned and waiting . . .

Time: 0858; a bright, spanking clear morning; sunlight shimmering on a flat calm sea. At the sound gear, a sailor suddenly tenses as the throbbing beat of enemy propellers begins to come through over his headphones. (*Gudgeon* is at Battle Stations, with "Jumping Joe" Grenfell in the control room talking things over with Lieutenant H. B. Lyon, his navigator and exec.)

"Captain to the conning tower!" the squawk box abruptly erupts.

The summons is academic. For Grenfell is only a few feet below the sound man and with the very first syllable, he takes the tower ladder like a monkey with a hotfoot. In seconds, he is standing beside the operator asking for range and bearing to target.

Below, the plotting party is fast getting a correct solution. There are new bearings being repeated. And the TDC (Torpedo Data Computer) operator is frantically cranking successive information into his console, to give the captain the correct firing angle. Throughout the boat, electric tension courses all compartments as telephone talkers relay "the poop" that an enemy warship is coming into the periscope and "the Old Man is lining 'er up!"

Then, from Grenfell in the battle-lighted conning tower:

"Open the outer doors!"

A slight thump is felt as the forward torpedo

room makes ready the bow tubes. Another terse whisper from Grenfell, whose body rises slowly from a crouch with the elevation of the sub's periscope. At fifty-five feet, only a few inches of the 'scope show above the unruffled surface of the Pacific. The captain sucks in his breath. The setup is beautiful! The Jap is coming down the track big as life itself! White-uniformed officers and lookouts are on the bridge enjoying the morning!

The target continues to close...and it is now finally 0908. A short check with TDC and then:

"Fire One! Fire Two! Fire Three!"

Gudgeon goes deep as torpedoes streak from her tubes. And she is still there as timed explosions suddenly echo through the hull, closely followed by breaking up noises and escaping air. It is all over.

Again, Grenfell calls for periscope depth. On top, the sea is barren. There is nothing left of the I-boat. There is only sky and water and debris...

The year 1942 was one of trial and error, of bitter disappointment in the torpedo's efficacy, of hits that never quite scored, and of an enemy who, nevertheless, was rapidly developing a healthy respect for U.S. submarines and their daring. Among these was Lieutenant Commander William H. Brockman's *Nautilus*, one of the picket line positioned for the Japanese attack on Midway. Although his fish failed to explode on contact, Brockman—despite the best efforts of the IJN—sent three torpedoes at the damaged aircraft carrier *Soryu*, and at first glance, believed that he had sunk her.

Three months later, on August 9, 1942, the United States Navy's amphibious invasion of the Solomon Islands became a *fait accompli* as Marines landed on Guadalcanal and Tulagi to open the campaign in the South Pacific. The Japanese reacted violently, sending down a task force of cruisers and destroyers from Rabaul to oust the invasion. And they did, very

nearly. The invasion hung by a thread as Admiral
Gunichi Mikawa's task force caught the Navy flat-
footed and, in twenty-three minutes of murderous
fire, sent four Allied heavy cruisers to the bottom.

The following morning, however, Lieutenant Commander J. R. Moore's S-44, the only American submarine in the area, was on hand to greet the enemy
cruiser *Kako* as she returned to base. This was small
compensation for the defeat at Savo, of course, but
it was something the complacent Japanese would
never forget: where there were American submarines, there was always trouble. And there were
American submarines everywhere!

Off Kavieng Harbor, New Ireland, the old S-boat
(850 tons, built as part of the Navy's World War
I program) was on her third war patrol out of Bris-
bane, Australia. Stationed in an area of heavy Japanese traffic, Moore expected business but nothing
quite so bountiful as befell the leaky, senescent
S-44 at 0750 on August 10.

While the Japanese were cleaning up their warships' bright-work and scrubbing down decks for a
glorious entry to port, Moore stuck up the S-boat's
periscope and noted two cruisers coming toward him
out of the early morning sun. Range was nine thousand yards. Moore swung the periscope as his OOD
rang up battle stations, and S-44 wheeled into action.

Then two more cruisers (heavy) hopped into the
periscope, line of bearing 45 degrees relative. The
enemy warships were riding in two columns. Moore
noted destroyers between. After a few moments of
thought, Moore decided to attack the rear ship of the
far column, and gave orders to his approach party
accordingly.

Five minutes later, S-44 was on firing course. The
first column of cruisers steamed by. Then the first of
the second column. Finally, at 0808, the last heavy
cruiser closed the range to only seven hundred yards.
So close was the doughty S-boat that her skipper

could see Japanese officers using binoculars on *Kako*'s bridge.

"Fire One! Fire Two! Fire Three! Fire Four!" Moore hissed, and a moment later, *"Take 'er deep— 130 feet!"*

Even before the submarine was down to her desired depth, eight thousand tons of enemy heavy began to break up as thunderous explosions echoed through the hull.

All torpedoes hit...

"Evidently her boilers blew up," Moore said in the aftermath. "You could hear hideous noises that sounded like steam hissing through water. Those noises were more terrifying to the crew than the actual depth charges that followed. It sounded as if giant chains were being dragged across our hull, as if our own water and air lines were bursting."

Vengeance for Savo gave American submarines their first major IJN warship of World War II.

But with the good, there came the bad—the first submarines "overdue and presumed lost." Nevertheless, there was more good news than bad as the year waned. And the following year, even more than the previous one.

By December 3, 1943, when Lieutenant Commander R. E. M. Ward's *Sailfish* struck terror into Japanese hearts with the sinking of escort carrier *Junyo* in a typhoon, the tide of war had long begun to change.

The following stanzas constitute Ward's own account of the night ex- *Squalus* came into her own:

1745: Surfaced in typhoon weather. Tremendous seas, forty to fifty knot wind, driving rain, and visibility, after twilight, varying from zero to five hundred yards.

2348: Radar contact bearing 114 T (154 relative), range 9,500 yards. Commenced tracking (ship contact #1).

2351: Estimated target course 320 T, speed eighteen knots.

2352: Radar contact on another and smaller target just to right of and about 900 yards closer than first contact.

2353: Radar contact on a third target about the same size as first contact and located about one thousand yards beyond first contact.

2355: Radar contact on fourth target smaller than other contacts and nine hundred yards closer than number two contact.

2356: Have still only managed to build up speed to twelve knots since initial contact. With these fast targets at close range, have abandoned any idea of methodical approach, the seas are mountainous with a driving rain. Can't see a thing but blackness and water with the water mostly in my face.

2358: Came left to 300°T to get off the track of the near target (believed to be a destroyer).

0000: Near target close aboard on starboard quarter turned on what appeared to be a good size search-light with a greenish tinge to it, directed at us and apparently signaling. He could not have seen us so assume he was signaling to someone else near us or he had a doubtful radar contact.

0001: Dove to forty feet and came right to course 340°T for bow shot at biggest pip. We are four hundred yards off track of near destroyer. All targets seem to be in line of bearing, roughly 280-100 degrees true with 900-1,000 yards between targets. Although initial radar contact was not made until a range of 9,500 yards, the picture looks as though we are on the left flank of a fast group of men of war, consisting of a destroyer, then possibly a cruiser, then a carrier or battleship, then another carrier or battleship with possibly something beyond that. Selected nearest of two largest pips as our target.

0009: Nearest destroyer passing close aboard to starboard and ahead.

0012: Fired tubes one, two, three and four, by radar setup, range 2,100 yards, gyro angle 53° to 37° right, track 108 to 120 port, torpedoes set at twelve feet, using spread of 1 3/c° right, 1 3/4° left, 5° right. Times of hits indicate torpedoes one and four were hitting torpedoes. Commenced swinging left to bring stern tubes to bear. Heard two torpedoes hit.

0016: Two depth charges fairly close. Went deep and started crossing astern of target.

0017 to

0152: Nineteen depth charges, some very close. Completed reload.

0158: Surfaced and commenced running up target track to intercept possible cripple. Unable to make much speed without shipping black water.

0230: Radar contact bearing 310°T, range 8,400 yards. Commenced tracking.

0240: Tracking shows target to be circling. The pip is small, yet can't believe radar would pick up a destroyer at 8,400 yards tonight. Commenced easing in slowly. At times the pip has an edge on it giving a momentary indication of another target very close to the one we are tracking.

0430: Target settled down on a northwesterly course, speed two to five knots. Radar pip now looks like we may have two targets very close together.

0550: Morning twilight and visibility improving fast, rain has stopped, but bridge is still shipping water, targets tracking with speed varying from one to three knots, range 3,500 yards. With visibility improving so rapidly

must fire soon, hence have decided to fire
three bow tubes on the surface and then attack again in daylight by periscope, making
reload during approach.

0552: Fired tubes one, two, and three, range 3,200
yards, gyros 002°, 00-1/2°, estimated track
148° starboard, TDC speed one knot, torpedoes set at ten feet, spread of 0°, ½° right,
and ½° left.

0557: Observed and heard two torpedo hits. First
hit looked like a momentary puff of fire, second hit looked like and sounded (on the
bridge) like a battleship firing a broadside—
even with the locomotive rumble so characteristic of sixteen inch shells. Commenced
swinging ship to bring stern tubes to bear in
case target started going elsewhere.

0558: The Nips started celebrating by firing star
shells and heavy AA tracers from at least a
dozen guns located at the point of the torpedo
explosions, but didn't seem to know where
we were because the shooting was directed
every place but toward us. It's a good shot
but despite the illumination I can't see the
target.

0600: Tracers coming our way now—plenty of them.

0601: Submerged. Commenced checking torpedoes
and reloading.

0603 to

0605: Four depth charges not near us.

0748: Finally see something—*Aircraft Carrier,
range about ten thousand yards,* dead in
water. Nothing else in sight. Impatiently continued check of torpedoes. All tubes were
flooded during each preceding attack. Gyro
pots of one torpedo aft and one forward are
flooded necessitating reload.

The escort carrier, Chuyo, *was indeed dead in the*

*water, the end result of a good night's work. But
there was still a lot of water between herself and
the bottom of the Pacific. Ward's work, in short,
was not done...*

0748: Momentarily sighted tops of a destroyer
(*Urakaze*) apparently standing by the carrier.
The picture now indicates that we have a
badly damaged carrier plus one destroyer. If
there were a cruiser here with eighty-five
foot tower and 125 foot mast he'd show up
like a sore thumb compared to the carrier's
sixty foot flight deck. Depth control is extremely difficult due to mountainous seas.
When we are at sixty feet there is nothing
but green water with the scope looking into
or under a wave most of the time. At fifty-
five feet we damn near broach and still can
only see about 20 percent of the time. I am
convinced that the carrier is a dead duck
but there should be someone else around beside a single destroyer, yet there is nothing
in sight from fifty-five feet and no screws on
sound. Am passing carrier down port side
from aft forward, range about 1,500 yards.
He has many planes on deck forward and
enough people on deck aft to populate a fair
size village. The only visible evidence of previous hits is a small list to port and a small
drag down by the stern. The number of people on deck indicates they are prepared to
abandon ship—a reassuring picture.

0940: Fired tubes five, six, and seven, TDC range
1,700 yards, gyros 182° 185 3/4°, track 88
port, torpedoes set at twelve feet, using a
spread of 0°, 8° right and 2° left. All torpedoes heard running normal.

0942: Two hits (only one of these actually struck
the target at the end of a 2,700 yard run)

heard on sound and throughout the boat, followed by a very heavy swish on sound then
by exceptionally loud breaking up noises
heard not only on sound but also very clearly
throughout the boat. Although I had periscope up anticipating the pleasure of watching the hits, depth control was so lousy that
we were at sixty feet when the torpedoes hit
and all I could see when the scope was out of
the waves was a skyful of tracers being shot
up into the air from the carrier's bearing.
Ordered right full rudder and came to seventy
feet to come around for bow shots. Can't
figure how I made the range. Have been using a carrier's flight deck height of sixty
feet on the stadimeter.

0944 to
0945: Two depth charges not too far away.
0950: Completed turning. Still hear the breaking up
noises.
0951: At fifty-five feet for a look. Nothing in sight
on, or either side of, generating bearing. Made
sweep to look for the destroyer and sighted a
heavy cruiser of the Takao or Nachi Class.
Commenced swinging hard left to bring bow
tubes to bear.

0952: Angle on the bow 10 starboard and he is still
swinging toward, range 3,500 yards. Between
my surprise at having underestimated the
range of the carrier (2,700 yards instead of
1,700), the fairly close depth charges from a
destroyer I still hadn't been able to see, the
surprise sighting of the cruiser racing our
way with her forefoot showing over the
waves, and the boat starting to broach with
her left full rudder, I ordered ninety feet and
thus threw away the chance of a lifetime.
Picked him up on sound and attempted to

get ping range on the QC head. Turn count on JK head of 220, indicating eighteen knots. By the time data was obtained from sound to allow even a chance of a hit he was astern and fading out fast. The Monday morning quarterbacks can have a field day on this attack!... This cruiser was undoubtedly on the off bow of the carrier.

0954 to
1004: Seven depth charges not too close. Destroyer screws fading in and out. Keeping them abaft the beam.

1330: Periscope depth. A careful fifteen minute look at depths between fifty-two and sixty feet reveals nothing. I am convinced the carrier had been sunk and the cruiser had gotten clear.

1400: Set course to proceed to area.

2400: One full day's work completed.

Struck by *Sailfish's* third torpedo at 0940, the escort carrier promptly went down.

This attack, characterized by Japanese Admiral Miwa as "a striking example of what submarines can accomplish by relentless and persistent attacks," is symbolic of the personal courage and unremitting determination that it took to best a skilled enemy.

The U.S. submarine force—in the first two years of the war alone—accounted for 73 percent of Japanese shipping losses and over a four-year spread, 54.7 percent of the enemy's merchant fleet, plus 29 percent of her naval vessels ...

The following stories will afford the reader an opportunity to see for himself what it took—the calibre of men, the ships, the *esprit de corps*—to win.

SEARAVEN

AT BATTLE STATIONS, the submarine *Searaven* moved slowly off the coast of Timor, NEI, nosing into the line of beach. It was a clear, warm night, sea calm, a scimitar moon firing the crests of breakers several hundreds yards away.

With well-rehearsed precision, four sailors emerged from the forward torpedo room and uncoupled two small wooden boats secured topside. Moments later, the submarine stopped.

On the darkened bridge that April 11, 1942, a commanding voice growled into a speaker tube: "Where the hell's Cook? What's holding him up?"

Somebody replied: "Captain, I sent a messenger down to the wardroom. He's getting ready now."

Throughout the American fleet boat, electric tension gripped the crew as all hands abruptly realized that a large Jap force was ashore, and shore was uncomfortably close now. In the periscope shears, four lookouts with night binoculars scanned the island for signs of life. Below them, a small group of officers anxiously watched the main induction hatch. The skipper was Commander Hiram Cassedy, a former Annapolis linesman. Beside him stood the exec, Lieutenant Commander Frank Walker.

Cook appeared and Cassedy acidly asked: "Where you been, boy? In the sack?"

Ensign George Carlton Cook grinned. He was twenty-four, a reservist from Milton, Massachusetts, a tall, rangy kid who invariably volunteered for any kind of hazardous duty. Cook told the captain: "No, in the control room, sir. Checking that map again—"

Dry said: "Check your watch, Cook. It's exactly eleven-forty—you sure you know the recognition signals?"

"Yes, sir."

"Okay, Cook. No damned hero crap. You just find our Aussies and get the hell back here."

"Shove off, Cook," Cassidy grunted laconically. He offered his thick hand. "Good luck, boy."

Cook saluted, hurrying back to the cigarette deck and dropping down the ladder to the main deck. Forward, the four sailors had lowered gently into the seaway. Cook hurried forward, climbed over the side and down the limber holes and jumped into the boat. He grabbed the paddles and grinned.

"Good luck!" a man whispered.

Cook made a V with his fingers. Then he cast off and began rowing toward the beach. In Cook's pockets were compass, flashlight and batteries, extra .45 clips, and a waterproof packet of sulpha powder. On his right hip was his Colt. He had no special fears.

The set of the tide was stronger than Cook anticipated. By the time he was outside the farthest breakers, sweat was rolling down his back. He shifted his taut body for better positioning and dug in with every ounce of strength. The breakers were steep and the boat careened violently. By the time it was out of the surf's pull, Cook was soaked and the little craft almost full of water. Wearily, the ensign flung himself out of the craft, dragged it by the towline through the wash to the beach.

For a few moments, Cook crouched at the water's

edge breathing hard, trying to get his bearings. He swiveled around and looked at the dark silhouette of the *Searaven* beyond the line of breakers. Only her superstructure showed. Cook thought of the warm control room. Then his mind spun back to the problem of the moment. He had only seventy-five minutes, from start to finish, to find thirty-three Australians who'd been stranded on Timor since the Japs came.

Cook jerked the Colt out and began walking. Directly in front of him was a high dune, the top fringed by the jungle. He sucked in his breath and started up. At the top, he pulled out his compass and stood watching the flickering needle for a reciprocal direction. Then he began his search for the Australians.

It was fully fifteen minutes, moving through dense underbrush and jungle vines, before Cook saw anything. When he did, he made just one mistake: he turned on his flashlight and poked the beam upward to shine on his face. About forty feet from where he stood, a group of a dozen Australians were sitting around a campfire. Cook shouted:

"Hey, you guys! Let's go! I'm an American submarine officer—"

Instantly, the ragged band of men scattered. Cook searched around. Nothing. No one. Despondent and frustrated, he backtracked to the beach and his boat. After paddling twenty minutes, he came alongside the submarine took a line and swung aboard. He reported to the bridge:

"I found a bunch of scary guys sitting at a campfire," he told the skipper. "When they saw me, they hightailed it out of there."

Cassedy expressed neither surprise nor anger. Dismissing the obviously disappointed young ensign for the moment, he spat out the orders that reversed the submarine and sent her running for deep water on four main engines. It had been a good try that simply didn't pay off, but it was only the first try They would be back, Cassedy told the exec. He vowed to return as many nights as were necessary, and his men knew that he would. By then, George Carlton Cook was down below in the wardroom, wearing dry khakis and waiting for an informal interrogation by his CO over black coffee.

The third war patrol for *Searaven* was the first for young Cook. In January, after a mission to Corregidor, Cassedy torpedoed his first ship—a 5,600 ton freighter off Manila. Then came more "special missions" despite Cassedy's belligerent requests to go to war. He wanted to fire fish and not being permited to do so, until these missions were completed, became a hard man on his junior officers. And that included Ensign Cook.

Cook came aboard in Australia, a tall, sinewy kid, fresh out of Massachusetts Nautical School, with a gaunt expression and deep-set blue eyes. He told the skipper of the *Searaven* that he didn't particularly care what jobs were tossed to him, just so long as he had a chance to fight. Cassedy took him at his word.

Cook's seagoing background in the Merchant Marine made him uniquely valuable as an ensign. He was able to stand watch at sea, as well as fill the odious duty of commissary and assistant engineering officer. Whatever there was to be done, young Cook did it and happily. When the rescue of the stranded thirty-three Aussies from the beach at Timor came up, Cassedy had his man . . .

The captain's interrogation in the wardroom was brief and informal. Cook told his story and Cassedy made pertinent notes, after which the skipper dismissed the ensign from all duties for the day and told him to get two volunteers to help out in the evening when *Searaven* surfaced again. Cook was disappointed, but he understood Cassedy's position.

"What kind of men?" he asked glumly.

"Single and strong," Cassedy said tersely. "If we

don't get these Aussies, we'll never get out on war patrol!"

"That's all, Captain?"

"Yeah," Cassedy grunted. "And next time don't shout. Just walk up to 'em. You can't blame those guys for being jittery."

All day the submarine remained submerged, lying off the coast along the sealanes. Nothing steamed by. Cook killed time first by sleeping, then going forward to the torpedo room and looking over his prospective volunteers. After dark, when the *Searaven* surfaced and ran in to the coast of Timor, George Carlton Cook made his choice: a torpedoman striker named C. L. Cook and Joseph L. McGivney, a soundman second class. Both men were thoroughly briefed and outfitted. Then, with Cook, they reported to the captain.

"No shouting, no noise of any kind," Cassedy told them. "Find those guys and bring 'em back . . ."

At 11:45 P.M., the submarine hove to off the breakers. Again lookouts in the shears reported no sign of life on the beach. Cook and his volunteers were called to the bridge. The three men took their final instructions and went down to the main deck to board the boat. McGivney took the stern seat, Carl Cook the bow, and the ensign grabbed the paddles.

They were parallel to the beach and just outside the breakers when George Cook said: "There was a good surf running last night and there's a good one again. If we spill out of the boat, try to grab a rung and hold on—the pull will drag you down—"

Then the boat was suddenly bouncing over the crest of the first wave. The rise was almost vertical and the descent was just as bad. The second was worse and the third did it. A long wave that broke prematurely, it tipped the little boat and sent its occupants sprawling into the wash. But the three men came up feet first and, holding fast to the rungs, managed to get firm footing and be pushed to

the shallows. Sopping wet, they dragged the boat into
the shadows on the beach.

Ensign Cook whispered: "The jungle's up the
dune, that's where I saw 'em. Ready now?"

The two sailors nodded and George Cook swiveled
around. Two minutes later, the three men stood at
the edge of the jungle. The ensign watched the needle
of his compass, then remarked softly:

"From now on, you're on your own: Be back here
in twenty-five minutes. That's all the time we're
allowed."

He took the center position; McGivney and C. L.
Cook, the flanks. They spaced out at one hundred
yards and at a signal (the ensign whistled softly)
started walking inland. George Carlton Cook knew
his responsibility well. This time he had no intention of letting the Aussies run away. If anybody did
the running, he swore, it was going to be him chasing the stranded men.

Bulling his way through the jungle brush, Cook
stumbled on a narrow trail and decided to follow it
inland. At the spot where he'd come across the camp-
site the night before, there was nobody, nothing.
He stopped and risked detection by shining his light
for a second over the cold, charred wood. Then he
began walking again.

He was perspiring fiercely and swatting clouds of
mosquitoes that followed him through the deadwood.
Ever so often, he'd stop and listen. Off in the distance, his two men were searching around and once
in a while he'd hear one slap at the mosquitoes.
Other than that there was nothing, no evidence that
anyone, Japanese included, was anywhere around.
But the jungle was all embracing and secretive. It
wasn't until Cook had covered a couple of miles that
the jungle let down its barriers, sufficiently for him
to hear movement.

He heard it from a long distance and he crouched,
gun up, waiting. He waited a precious five minutes

and then slowly began walking again. The brush ahead crackled abruptly as someone tread softly on dead wood. Cook jumped back into the bushes, took the Colt off safety, and sucked in his breath.

Instinct told him that whoever was approaching was not a Japanese and not one of his men back-tracking. He put the safety back on and reversed the gun, squinting along the faintly moonlit trail until he saw the outline of a man. Cook pulled back his arm and cocked it. The man came on slowly, as if listening to his every step. When he was nearly paral-lel, Cook stopped breathing and waited to see the shadowed face. He let his breath out in a wild rush of air and the man swiveled frantically.

"Hold it, mister!" Cook hissed. "I'm not about to chase you guys tonight."

The Australian was an officer, tall, cadaverous. He stammered. *"W-who are you?"*

"The same guy who found you last night, kobber." Cook emerged from the bushes and extended his hand. "George Carlton Cook from the submarine *Searaven.* Now, please, for Crissakes, where the hell are your men?"

"Gitt, Lieutenant L. B. Gitt, Australian Army," the other said automatically. "The men are on the other side of the lagoon."

"How far?"

"Mile or two, the most."

"Let's go—*run,* Lieutenant! We've got just so much time on the beach."

Gitt ran.

Leading the way along a trail glutted with dead-falls, the Australian raced straightaway for his camp with Cook following. Twelve of the precious twenty-five minutes had elapsed by the time the Australian stopped, wheezing and holding up one bony hand.

"They're probably tucked away in the trees," he grinned. "You know, old man, you can hear a long way in this jungle—"

"What happens now?" Cook asked impatiently.

The Aussie shoved two fingers between his lips and whistled long and low. He let five seconds elapse and repeated the identification process. Then he said: "Come on, Yank. Nobody'll cut your throat now."

The two men walked through a seemingly impenetrable wall of vines and into a darkened clearing. There, the rest of the thirty-three Australians came out and surrounded Cook and pumped his hand warmly.

"No questions now, gents," Cook hissed. "We have to make that beach in twelve minutes."

"We've got several sick men!" somebody whispered.

Cook stared over the ragged band and nodded. "Okay!" he snapped. "Carry 'em!"

Then he turned on his heel, motioning for Gitt to lead the way out. Carrying their sick and wounded in litters hacked from the jungle, the caravan of half-starved Australians—the remnants of the garrison at Timor—arrived at the beach in the allotted time. Cook hadn't given any thought to their transportation to the submarine, but as the thirty-three of them (and the two assisting sailors who had returned by now) grouped silently around the wooden boat, the ensign devised a plan: first out would be the litter cases, shuttled back and forth until all had reached safety, then the rest of them would leave by boat through the surf.

Stripping off his sweat-soaked shirt, Cook swiveled around to Gitt and muttered: "You jump in and paddle. The rest of us will get these basket cases in around you. I'll swim alongside."

Gitt protested, "You're liable to get killed."

Cook said, "I doubt it. Anyway, if we ever get to the sub somebody's got to bring the boat back."

The first of three litter cases was placed gently aboard. The Aussie lieutenant climbed in and the boat was launched. Cook removed his trousers and dropped them on the sand He nodded. Eager hands walked the rubber boat and its occupants to deep water. Nobody had mentioned the likelihood of being discovered by Japanese soldiers, but the thought was present in everyone's mind, particularly Cook's.

Carl Cook had waded to deep water with the ensign and now he stood beside the young officer in the chest-high water, worried for the safety of the Australians.

"Want me to swim alongside too?" he asked.

The ensign shook his head. "No, you get the hell back to the beach and form some kind of guard. Tell the Aussies they'll have to protect themselves if the Japs show."

"Mister Cook," the torpedoman doggedly said, "you can use some help yourself. Please let me go along!"

"No dice. Get the hell back!"

Overhead, low-scudding clouds raced across the path of dim moonlight and shielded, for a moment, the movement of men through the surf. Then the clouds drifted by. Cook, breast-stroking through the first wave, his left hand holding the boat, took a mouthful of water when the wave broke prematurely, but doggedly forged ahead. Gitt, midships in the boat, dug in the paddles.

Cold sea thundered over Cook's head from every direction as the little boat twisted and veered crazily in the troughs. Over his shoulder, the ensign could see the emaciated Australian grimly working his paddles. Over his shoulder, too, Cook could see the knot of men on the beach watching anxiously as the rubber boat bounced in the seaway.

The second and third waves of this first trip to *Searaven* were uniformly difficult. Cook fought the pull of the surf until his right arm felt like it would fall off, then reversed his hold and led the craft from the opposite swimming position. At last the boat was out of the surf.

"Out there! All right?" Gitt called.

Cook nodded weakly and resumed the lead. Five minutes later the boat was chafing against the submarine and hands were gently lifting the Australians aboard. Cook told a chief gunner's mate:

"Tell the old man I need all the time I can get. They're on the beach now—all of 'em."

Grabbing a limber hole, George Cook pulled himself into the boat. Without other delay, except to catch his breath, Cook paddled through the surf. He repeated the process until only four Australians and his own men, C. L. Cook and Marion, were left on the beach.

Commander Cassedy had stretched the ensign's time ashore to get all the stranded men back to the submarine, but now streaks of gray were beginning to show in the eastern sky, and Cassedy had passed the word that *Searaven* could only wait for one last trip. Cook had to get them all now or else wait for another night.

Standing on the beach with the six men, Cook explained that the Americans would swim beside the boat while the four Australians paddled. Stripped to his waist, Cook glared at the surf. A wind had come up with the change of tide and the waves had suddenly heightened.

"We'll never make it through there, Mister Cook," Marion muttered. "It was bad enough before, but now it's damned near impossible."

"I know," Cook conceded. "But we've got to try, if we don't want to get stranded here."

Among the Australians, it was a toss-up who was strong enough to control the passage of the boat. A man named Sibley, a sergeant, grunted, "I'm weak as water, but I'm stronger than my men. Give me the paddles, sir."

Cook didn't argue. "Hop in. Take the midships

thwart. The rest of you men squeeze around. Shift your weight for balance. Let's go."

Pulled by the three Americans into deep water, the heavily burdened craft bobbed precariously in the wash. Sibley dug the paddles in, but the pull of.the tide had grown proportionately more severe as it had increased to full. The boat was going nowhere fast; if anything, it was going backward!

Cook grunted: "Sibley! Keep those guns handy and *paddle!*"

The three Americans had shed their weapons. They were deposited now in the lap of the Aussie sergeant. A shout came from the darkened beach. Sibley saw an enemy sentry pointing from the top of the dune. The bone-chilling spectacle was further enlivened by other shouts and then gun flashes.

"Paddle! For Chrissake paddle!" Cook yelled, gripping the bow ringbolt and tugging with every ounce of strength in his aching body. More frenzied shouts came from the beach. Looking around, Cook saw Japanese soldiers racing toward the water's edge. Yellow flashes of gunfire stabbed toward the little boat as it darted into the first wave.

Bullets smacking the water sent up small geysers around the submariners. Cook only had a glimpse of the Japanese soldiers lined up along the beach. The ensign's head was hit a glancing blow by the rubber boat as it careened wildly off a wave, and he slipped under, dazed, swallowing water. The boat bumped him again as he came up. He pushed to move it aside, but the motion of the sea held it over him.

Swimming underwater, his lungs straining, Cook bobbed to the surface astern of the two other American sailors and shouted hoarsely for Sibley to dig in. Then the other swimmers grabbed the ensign and forced his hands onto a ringbolt. It was more than a minute before his head cleared and he could swim again. By now the Japs were firing in earnest, and the boat was entering another set of waves.

Behind the swimmers, Japanese soldiers were running into the water, wading chest-deep for more accurate firing. Bullets whined around Sibley, alternately paddling and firing back. As quick as one of the guns was empty, Sibley threw it overboard and grabbed another. His firing counted heavily. Screams of agony fused with shouts of exhortation from the shore.

Abruptly, a .25 rifle bullet tore into Sibley's throat. He gagged silently and slumped over, losing a paddle. Instantly the sea caught the rubber boat and flipped it over. Cook dived underwater as a body bumped against him. He grabbed a shirt, took the man in a cross-chest carry, brought the man to the surface.

"Hold on! Hold on and you'll help me, soldier!" Cook shouted.

There were other screams of instruction as the U.S. Navy men helped the Australians. The group, minus Sibley, worked its way through the third set of waves and pushed out weakly through the rim of the surf.

On the deck of the submarine, a machine gun suddenly began spitting at the beach. Japanese soldiers twisted around, raced for the safety of the upper dune. It was all over, except for the backbreaking job of getting the Australians aboard. Willing hands relieved Ensign Cook and his two exhausted men of this job.

Searaven was underway as Cook flopped weakly on the deck and tried to grab a stanchion. He fell back and was helped to his feet, then raced with the others to the safety of the hatch. Sporadic shots from the beach fell wide of the little knot of men on the main deck. Cook grinned weakly at his two volunteers and the three men went below. Number of men rescued: thirty-two.

Ensign George Carlton Cook was the man of the hour aboard the *Searaven*. Commander Cassedy showed his appreciation of the success of the mission

with more than a well done speech. Cook received
the Navy Cross for extraordinary heroism when the
submarine arrived in Fremantle at the end of the
patrol. Then the *Searaven* went back to sea and sank
ships.

Cook was all for that. After Timor, conventional
torpedo warfare was a piece of cake.

SCUTTLE!

ON THE BRIDGE of the *Grenadier*, Lieutenant Commander John A. Fitzgerald, USN, stared intently at a two-ship Japanese convoy running Lem Valon Strait between the Malay Peninsula and Sumatra. It was eight-thirty on April 21, 1943; a hot, bright morning with only a slight cross-chop rippling the surface of the Indian Ocean.

"Radar range!" Fitzgerald snarled into the voice tube.

"Nine miles, Captain," came the report from Radioman 1/c Edward L. Poss, a moment later.

Fitzgerald nodded at the J-1 telephone talker standing at his elbow. "Tell the forward torpedo room to stand by," he said.

Then the Missouri-born [Annapolis '31] submariner pressed a pair of binoculars to his red-rimmed eyes and studied the enemy vessels again. At his side were Lieutenant Edward L. Whiting, *Grenadier's* executive officer and the OOD, Lt. K. T. Harty. The three men had been on the bridge since two-thirty when radar contact had been established. Closing at twenty knots from an impossible range, they had remained on top throughout the hunt. Now it was virtually over and an electric tension coursed through the boat; they were going in.

"Starboard Jap," Whiting droned, "looks worried. Bastard's starting to zigzag all over the drink."

Harty put his glasses on the target vessel. "You're right, but a fat lot of good it'll do him."

Fitzgerald made no immediate comment. His eyes were measuring the distance of the closest merchantman. He was turning over a few basic problems of command connected with the success of a daylight torpedo attack—problems inherent in a case where a sub has already been sighted. What was his effective torpedo range? What were the target angles, if any? Should he, as was suggested earlier, use his 3-inch deck gun to sink them both? Was an end-around possible, running ahead of the Japs and then submerging with torpedoes ready? The two-and-a-half striper had only to stare at the calm sea to dismiss his last thought.

"Ask the tower to give us a fathometer reading, son," he instructed the J-1 talker. Then, as the sailor was passing this order, Fitzgerald turned to his exec and OOD. "Before we end up chasing the bastards clear to dry land, I want to know where the hell bottom is."

Whiting spat over the side and glanced over for an instant. "Last look I had at the chart, Captain, it was about 400 feet."

"It was about half that when I looked," Fitzgerald said softly. He turned impatiently to the talker. "What's the poop?"

The sailor shrugged, pressing the button and asking for a reading again. But in a moment he was all frowns. "Sir," he said, "the control room says the fathometer must've kicked out. They can't get a reading."

Fitzgerald whirled and raced back to the conning tower ladder. He dropped into the hole and shortly was standing in the control room, breathing down the back of an electrician rating who was repairing the set. He glanced at the Diving Officer, Lt. H. H. Sherry.

"Mac, since when has this thing been out of whack?"

"Just now, Captain."

"What was your last reading?"

"Short of a hundred fathoms."

Fitzgerald swore softly. "Goddammit, Sherry, we're sitting ducks out here. Get that thing in running order and report your depth."

"Yes, sir." Sherry turned to the electrician. "How long do you figure?"

The sailor shrugged.

Then, disgustedly, Fitzgerald grabbed the bridge ladder and clambered back aloft. On top, Whiting and Harty were both studying the enemy vessels with their glasses. The ships were closer, but spaced out.

"Come right to 155 degrees," Fitzgerald boomed into the tube. "Control, what are we making now?"

"Almost twenty-one, Captain."

The Missourian frowned. He still had not determined the precise attack approach, nor could he do so correctly unless he knew his depth.

"Control, what's with the fathometer?"

"Not yet, Captain."

Fitzgerald swiveled around and walked back to the periscope shears. There were four blue jackets hanging in them, scanning the bright East Indian sky with binoculars. He started to admonish them with the usual words, *Keep 'em wide open, men. We're well within the range of land-based Jap bombers.* But the words stuck in his throat.

Suddenly, above him, the after lookout tensed and his right index finger shot out stiffly. He yelled:

"Aircraft! Port quarter!"

Grenadier's skipper catapulted forward to the voice tube.

"There's an aircraft coming in on the port quarter! Have you got it down there?"

"Yes, sir," reported Poss, an instant later. "He's at sixteen thousand yards, sir—"

Fitzgerald brought up his glasses and immediately picked up the speck in the sky. He cursed softly and his stomach did flip-flops. His exec and OOD were also bemoaning their luck. A plane meant quick submergence and that meant a probable loss of targets. But there was no question in his mind as to what he had to do. For long moments he studied the target until spotting the first glimmer of a four-motored Kawanichi bomber. Then he lowered the glasses and let out a deep sigh.

"All right," he boomed, "clear the bridge! *Dive! Dive!*"

The raucous blasts of the alarm commenced on the last word. There was a mad scramble as lookouts, bridge talker and three officers tore into the hole. The last man down was Fitzgerald, and as he plunged down the hole, *Grenadier* was already flooding with a 15 degree down angle.

"Mister Sherry, come to 150 feet and level off!" he bellowed as the hatch banged shut above his head.

In the control room, the plotting party was hunched around the table beginning to chart the two targets. In the forward torpedo room, all tubes had been secured but the sailors were waiting tensely for orders to open outer doors. Throughout the boat, men turned their thoughts to the man in the tower giving the orders. And throughout the boat there was only one thought: *what about those Japs—would they still be around to pickle when the surface alarm was blown?*

John Anthony Fitzgerald, one-time Annapolis boxing team captain, thought not. But deep within him was the lingering hope that somehow he could pick up the scent. It all depended on how long the Kawanichi bomber kept them pinned down.

"Sound," Whiting growled beside him, "keep check

on those merchantmen. We're going upstairs one of these days."

"Lieutenant Sherry says we're passing one hundred feet by depth indicator and still diving, Captain!" reported the J-1.

"Very well."

It was hot and dank in the conning tower, and the only sound was the eerie pinging on the two enemy ships as they fled for the sanctuary of Sebang harbor. For the men who waited there, waiting for Japanese bombs to drop, it was a long, insufferable moment. But it was par for the course.

Grenadier was not a particularly lucky submarine. She had never been in any life or death struggles with Japanese convoys. Under Fitzgerald, now making his second patrol in command [*Grenadier's* sixth], the best torpedo score to date was the crippling of two 14,000 tonners and a number of spitkits. In fact, hunting had been so poor during the first ten days of the sixth patrol that the Missourian actually broke radio silence to request a new operating area. This area held game—or so it appeared until the Japanese patrol bomber.

"Passing 120 feet, Captain," the voice of the J-1 talker cut through Fitzgerald's reverie.

"Very well. Tell Mister Sherry to take her to 150 and level off. Is that fathometer working yet?"

The talker repeated the two-and-a-half striper's words. A few seconds later he frowned and said: "Not yet, Captain. Still working on it. It's a condenser or something."

Fitzgerald studied his stopwatch. It was more than a minute since the Portsmouth-built submarine had dipped under. He wasn't worried about the effect of the Kawanichi's bombs at this depth; he was thinking about the targets and the correct solution to use for their demise. He wiped the sheen of sweat from the folds of his neck and squatted beside the sound recorder.

"Still got 'em, Poss?"

"Loud and clear, Captain." The radioman gri-maced. "I wish to hell that Jap would make a play and clear out—"

Warranngg! Warranngg!

The deafening roar of two close-order explosions reverberated throughout the length and breadth of the submarine, instantly throwing her into a 15 de-gree starboard list and knocking out all power and light. In every compartment, officers and men dropped into a confused tangle of arms and legs as an uncontrolled *Grenadier* moved into the depths of Lem Valon Strait.

Desperately, savagely, Fitzgerald extricated him-self from the mass of humanity in the darkened con-ning tower and groped his way onto the ladder to the control room. A moment later, he was below racing toward the diving stand. Here, a sailor had thrown on the red battle-light and it limned the somehow in-tact depth indicator in stark relief: 167 feet and still spinning. Everything else in the compartment was a wreck, and half-naked, frantic men were moving amid a rain of popping gauges and light bulbs and cork insulation, trying to save the boat.

"All compartments," the Missourian thumbed the intercom, *"report your damage! On the double!"*

And the reports came back in staggering succes-sion, the most alarming of which was the word of a fire in the maneuvering room. Fitzgerald sped aft, leaving Whiting and CTM W. C. Withrow to assess the damage caused by the bomb explosions along the after compartments.

Fighting his way along the sweaty, canted deck, he bulled through the crew's quarters. He was about fifteen feet from the maneuvering room when he saw men streaming out between clouds of acrid yellow smoke.

Next he saw his chief engineer, Lt. Alfred J. Toulon, standing at the entrance of the watertight door trying to peer into the smoke. When the engineer spotted him, he shook his head in the negative.

"It's in the rheostats and panel, Captain. Leslie and Linder are in there with foamite!"

Smoke was billowing from the partially closed door—smoke with the distinctive odor of an electric fire. The Missourian shoved his head inside. Flames danced along one bulkhead. Two blue jackets huddled around a flame-shrouded figure swatting his clothes with their bare hands. In another corner of the smoke-filled compartment a half-choking sailor was crawling on his hands and knees trying to reach the watertight door. This terrible panorama continued for some moments until, finally, all had been removed and the burning compartment sealed.

Fitzgerald whirled around, pushing past Toulon and almost ran headlong into a grim-faced Chief Torpedoman Withrow.

"What's the dope?" he snapped. "How bad?"

"All reports aren't in yet, Captain, but it's plenty bad—"

And the chief of the boat proceeded to enumerate: starboard side of the after torpedo room dished in six inches; after tubes, main shafts, hull frames bent. Hull frames in the maneuvering room bent, an electric fire and the door to the after room sprung. The after loading hatch strongback was bent. In the engine room the damage was restricted to all hydraulic lines; all carried away. The shock mountings of the radio transmitter had unseated in the conning tower, but the radio was still operable. Damage was still being assessed, said the enlisted man, and it extended clear to the forward torpedo room. The worst of it, obviously, was in maneuvering where short circuits and a ruptured motor-controller gave rise to the crippling fire.

The damage reports were still streaming in to control when Fitzgerald and Withrow reached that compartment. By then, *Grenadier* had come to the end of her dive—270 feet—and was resting on the bottom. There was nothing to do except clean up the mess and wait for the fire to go out before surfacing. The submarine commander spoke reassuring words to his stunned crew over the intercom. He told them to hold fast. He told them that everything would be all right.

But in his heart, Fitzgerald knew that the words had no meaning. His targets were probably gone, he realized, and Japanese escorts were doubtless on their way out. Worse, in the maneuvering room, the buckled plates were accommodating the sea and that meant a flooded compartment unless the fire was smothered first.

So began the heroic attempt to save the submarine. Until nine-thirty that night, Fitzgerald kept his crew busy shielding electrical leads and trying to make fundamental repairs. The maneuvering room fires had finally been smothered, and to reduce the level of water between the electric motors, Fitzgerald organized a long bucket brigade to the forward torpedo room. From here, pumps carried the water to sea. Sailors and officers keeled over from heat prostration, from sheer exhaustion, but eventually they got *Grenadier* reasonably dry and operating at dead slow speed on one bent shaft. The signal to blow everything and surface was only the start of the final hell, the last gasp.

It was black and moonless when the submarine limped to the surface and lay wallowing in her own trough, unable to turn up more than 450 of the required 2,750 amperes. On deck, a gun crew spilled out but found that the breach mechanism of the 3-inch gun was inoperative. Fitzgerald accepted the news with characteristic equanimity. He was on the bridge with Whiting and a double complement of lookouts. He told his exec:

"Get up all the automatic weapons and small arms

you can find. If we're going to have a fight on our hands tomorrow, I want the best fight possible."

Whiting plunged down the hole and Harty, the OOD, came up from the tower. He stood silently beside *Grenadier's* skipper, watching the submarine's slow crawl toward the open sea. He turned and stared at the wide, phosphorescent wake for a long moment. The sound of the diesels, barely rumbling, echoed forward in the calm night. He heard the soft sibilance of the bow wave, telling him what he already sensed: *Grenadier* was through, almost. He looked at Fitzgerald and saw the grim determination etched on the granite jaws. He saw the wild, unwarranted hope burning in his skipper's slate-gray eyes. It was fitting and proper, Harty told himself, but he sensed that it was only a look and nothing more.

"You think they'll find us in the morning, Captain?" he said, instantly sorry that he asked the question.

"Probably," Fitzgerald replied. His voice was calm, almost soft. "Probably every damned destroyer this side of Singapore is on the way right now."

"I figured as much."

Fitzgerald faced him. "What are the men saying, Harty? Do they think I goofed?"

"Negative, Captain," the OOD replied, shaking his head. "Nothing like that, sir. They say it's just the breaks of the game—and that they're not out of the game yet."

The Missourian smiled sadly. "Let's hope not."

"Nice night," Harty said suddenly, hoping to change the subject. "All we need now is a couple of big fat targets!"

"And a couple of new diesels."

"I don't know, skipper. I'll bet Toulon gets us moving in good shape in a little while."

"Sure," Fitzgerald smiled sadly. "God looks after the helpless and the hopeless. I'm afraid we're a little of both, so save your breath." Then he studied the

young OOD and said, "But don't worry, son, we're
not dead quite yet. There's a lot of fight left in this
bucket."

The longest night wore on and Fitzgerald chose
to remain on the bridge throughout most of it. But
once he made a tour of the boat and spoke com-
forting, fighting words to the bluejackets who were
on watch. And once he went back to the engine rooms
to see how the repairs were coming. Otherwise, he
was the familiar figure on top—the lonely skipper
awake through the changing watches—his bare head
tucked down deep in his parka, his eyes ever rest-
lessly studying the sea.

By five o'clock, the situation below decks had
worsened and a bone-weary lieutenant Toulon reported to the bridge that repairs had failed. Fitzgerald fell back on his only alternative to augment the
speed of the submarine.

"Pass the word for all hands on watch to start rig-
ging a sail," he ordered. "And tell the chief of the
boat to report to me double quick."

Minutes later, in the forward torpedo room where
men had gathered from all parts of the submarine,
Torpedoman 1/c Neil A. Andrews and Pharmacist
1/c J. J. McBeth were instructing the group in the
sewing of canvas. Torpedo covers, tarpaulin from
spare parts and canvas seat coverings were cut and
fit in a rough pattern. While one half of the men
snipped, the other half sewed—a sail like none of
them had ever seen before. But a sail, nevertheless.

Fitzgerald said to big, grizzled Chief Withrow, "I
think you better prep everybody for a fight come
daylight. With our luck we're liable to be becalmed."

"They expect a fight, Captain," Withrow grinned
wryly. "And as far as the sail goes, they *hope* it
works, but none of 'em is willing to make book on
it—"

Fitzgerald nodded. He sniffed the gray-black dawn.
In a few minutes the sun would come out of the sea

and maybe enough breeze to keep their hopes alive.
Then the chief went down the hole and Fitzgerald
licked his index finger, feeling nothing more than
the chill of a waning night.

By six-thirty it was light. The breeze had fallen
away to a whisper and the sea was like molten glass,
the sunlight coruscating on the flat, empty surface
of Lem Valon Strait. Fitzgerald, adamantly, was still
on the bridge. He was perched on a jump seat behind
the conning tower fairwater, staring over the bow
at a strange sight: there was a working party of
half-naked, sweating bluejackets, stringing a patch-
quilt sail along the lower guy wires to the antenna
trunk.

"How's it look, Captain?" bawled one of the chiefs.

"Just great!" Fitzgerald smiled with unwarranted
enthusiasm. "You men will get us to the coast of
China yet—"

"The hell with the coast of China, skipper," someone else yelled. "Just let's clear this goddamn passage!"

"Amen, brother!" said another. "Out of your
mouth into God's ears."

But God wasn't listening that April day, and it
became manifestly clear when the sail went slack
after another forty-five minutes. By now, there was
a distinct land smell in the breathless morning and
combined with some late word from the engineering spaces ["rheostats still falling off, sir"] new ideas
came acropping on *Grenadier's* bridge. Whiting
wanted to sail to the nearest land, blow up the submarine and escape overland to China; Harty wanted
to stay and fight it out, maybe capturing a Jap
sampan and sailing to the nearest Allied base; and
Fitzgerald leaned toward the Whiting pipe dream,
but his mind was far from made up.

The agonizing process of watching the sail catch
a few puffs of wind and then seeing it go slack again
continued to shortly before eight o'clock. It was then

that the Missourian accepted the fact that *Grenadier* was finished; that he should scuttle as close to land as possible. This was their only chance as morning wore on and the likelihood of detection became greater. He looked over the pathetic sail at his forward 20-mm gun crew. He swiveled around and stared at the men on the cigarette deck, resolutely hunched over their 20s, 50 calibers and Thompson submachineguns. And then he leaned into the brass speaker tube, speaking decisively to the junior officer of the watch.

"All right, Mister, come about to new course one eight zero and tell the crew that we will abandon ship when I give the word."

There was no questioning from below. *Grenadier's* crew had long ago faced up to the grim facts of life. Now, as the conning tower passed the word, submariners raced to footlockers in the living spaces and cleaned out their valuables.

On the bridge, the mood was blacker yet as the submarine twisted on a southerly heading toward the Malay Peninsula. The sun beat down unmercifully and the wind fell away. So, too, the speed. Fitzgerald called the comm officer and instructed him to send a message to Fremantle, describing their condition and saying that he was preparing to abandon. Then he gave orders to destroy all confidential papers, code books, coding machine and maps, and everybody knew without being told that the last, irreparable step had been taken. It was precisely at this moment that a Japanese float plane appeared to underscore John Anthony Fitzgerald's anxiety. Almost simultaneously, lookouts spotted a large destroyer or light cruiser standing in across the strait from the northwest.

"*Here we go,*" Fitzgerald called to his gunners. "*Stand by! That plane comes in to effective range and then you blast the sonuvabitch. Not before—*"

On the forward 20-mm the gunner put it to his loader his own way.

"It's our last time at bat in this goddamn war. I swing for the fences, buddy."

The plane came in on the port quarter attempting a run up the port side. Hundred kilogram bombs were tucked conspicuously under its wings. When it was about a quarter of a mile away and at 65 degrees elevation, Fitzgerald thundered the commence firing order. A solid wall of flame erupted from the superstructure of the submarine. Accurate, devastating, tracer trails groped and found their target and pieces of fabric slewed into the bright sky. The plane roared over and bullets *chinked* along steel decks and then the plane was gone, veering off, wobbling toward the land, one of its bombs dropping harmlessly into the sea two hundred yards away.

Then, as it suddenly veered around and made another pass at the stricken submarine, Fitzgerald's machinegunners cut loose. Simultaneously, the Jap did too. Three men, one on the machinegun and two at the gun scuttles, screamed and slumped to the decks as blood gushed from their punctured bodies. But the man at the machinegun, Seaman 1/c James Livered, pulled himself back up to the gun and half cursing, half screaming, emptied his wildly chattering weapon at the plane.

All of *Grenadier's* hot gunners went wild, but only for a few moments. Suddenly Fitzgerald's voice was heard over the din of lusty cheers:

"All hands lay aft on the fantail!" he shouted, repeating the order to the J-1 talker who relayed it throughout the submarine. "Prepare to abandon ship!"

By now the enemy warship was about three miles away and not shooting. There was no need to. The conclusion was obvious as the submarine's crew poured up through the inductions and raced aft. In a few moments the casualties of the maneuvering room fire and the nonswimmers went overboard in rubber life rafts. Then the long, grim-faced ranks of officers and men. The last to go were Fitzgerald and Chief Withrow, the latter sprinting below decks to open the vents and scuttle.

Finally it was over and the two men stepped down the limber holes into the sea, striking out for a few frantic seconds to clear the downward pull of the submarine. *Grenadier* was sinking stern first, bow hanging in the air like some grotesque antedeluvian monster. Swimming side-by-side toward the rafts and the seventy other survivors, the Missourian and his chief-of-the-boat turned around in the water as a loud, eerie hissing sounded behind them. Escaping air and bubbling oil cascaded upward from the submarine for long, miserable moments. Neither man spoke, but merely treaded water and watched in abject misery as *Grenadier* took the plunge. From that moment, nothing seemed to bother Fitzgerald's crew —not even grinning Japanese sailors popping off their flashbulbs while circling the scene.

The enemy ship, a destroyer, rescued all hands and later removed them to prison camps on Honshu and Kobe.

Fitzgerald received the Navy Cross for this and his previous patrol in the ill-fated submarine, primarily because of his courage beyond the call of duty in an area which he himself voluntarily requested.

So ended *Grenadier's* life, one of fifty-two American submarines sunk in enemy waters by freak, close-order bombs from a Kawanichi. Many U.S. submarines survived such pummeling, and repeatedly, but John Anthony Fitzgerald's command was the exception that proved the rule about a pigboat's Achilles Heel.

THE DEFEATED

"Radar contact! Captain to the tower!"

The sudden, intrusive rasp of the wardroom squawkbox aboard the submarine USS *Sculpin*, instantly brought Navy Captain John P. Cromwell, SubDiv 43, and Commander Fred Connaway, boat skipper, to their feet. Charging through the forward battery, the two men scrambled up the conning tower ladder and, seconds later, stood breathlessly behind RT 2/c Edward M. Beidelman, watching a fast-filling 'scope.

As a wolfpack commander operating in the Gilbert Islands on the eve of the Marine attack on Tarawa, Cromwell, forty-two—handsome, aggressive—was official custodian of submarines *Sculpin*, *Searaven* and *Apogon*. Upon him rested responsibility for division and independent deployment. But from the standpoint of command, it was Fred Connaway, ten years Cromwell's junior, who ran the show during the sub's ninth patrol.

"What's your count, Beidelman?" The skipper's voice lashed the hushed darkness of the tower.

"Six pips, sir. Speed fifteen knots."

"Range?"

"Eighteen thousand yards, Captain. Base course two nine zero."

Connaway whirled on the division commander:

"Request permission, sir, to make a full-power run on that convoy!"

But Cromwell hesitated briefly. Although cut from the same cloth as his boat skipper, there were other considerations that November 19, 1943, at 0200 hours: ComSubPac of necessity, had entrusted him with a broad outline of Operation Galvanic [Tarawa] and related plans for the Navy's legups in the Gilberts and Marshalls. If Cromwell approved of the skipper's attack and that attack were not successful —what then? The division commander pursued the dark thoughts to their logical conclusion ... capture? Torture till the Japs made him spill everything? He considered the odds, the possible eventualities, then turned to Connaway.

"Let's roll," he said calmly. "Let's go sling some pickles before those bastards disappear—"

Responsively, the sub skipper whipped around to Lieutenant George E. Brown, the OOD, barking the order that sent *Sculpin* surging down a new bearing with four mains on the line.

"Hit that general alarm Brownie!" Connaway grated. *"All engines ahead full!"*

A moment later, the alarm rippled through the sub's compartments and eighty-four men sprinted to battle stations for night torpedo attack. Then Cromwell and Connaway bounded up the bridge ladder into the night.

Topside, it was calm and clear. In the periscope shears, four lookouts were squinting hard trying to spot the loom of a convoy ten miles distant. Connaway and his boss went over the general plan of attack: a full-power end-around that would find them logging more miles, but one which would put the submarine strategically in front of the onrushing Japs. Then, depending on the final setup in the TDC [Torpedo Data Computer] and convoy formation, the schedule called for opening of outer torpedo doors within the hour, quick submergence and the start of many shooting observations.

Below decks, too, officers were scheming: Lieutenant N. J. Allen, the exec, had whipped together the plotting party and was executing duties as navigator. Three or four officers were hunched over the chart table in the control room with slide rules, dividers, stop watches and area maps—all meticulously working for a successful end-around. Chief of the Boat Peter Gabrunas [CTM] was shuttling between torpedo rooms, checking out steam and electric fish in the spare racks.

The call to battle stations, meanwhile, had brought Lieutenant Brown to the bridge as gunnery officer, while Ensign John Gamel went to the tower as JOOD. Now the three officers stood silently together, each to his own thoughts as they stared out over the fair-water ... For Cromwell, these thoughts possibly centered on his calculated risk and the secret information that he, alone, possessed; for Connaway, these moments were for visualizing the possible setup and preparing for emergencies; and for Brown, they were for thinking of the countermeasures—battle surface —he's be ordering if anything went wrong.

But none of the three key officers on the bridge *really* suspected something might go wrong in the end-around; they merely considered the possibility and, once having mulled it, collectively threw the dice. The "191," a famous identifying number in sub circles, had been the boat which sighted *Squalus*' buoy that black day three years before off Portsmouth, N.H.—a buoy which eventually led to the rescue of forty-three submariners. *Sculpin*'s wartime career, however, had not to this time been a roaring success [only ten thousand Jap tons under Connaway, her sole wartime commander] so this probably accounted for her crew's fervor to go in and sink.

As the first minutes of the attack ticked off, the uncovered head of Ensign Bill Fiedler, the comm officer, popped through the hatch. He'd drafted and coded a contact report. Did Captain Connaway want to get it off?

"Negative!" Cromwell spoke up. "No transmitters now—they're too damned close! If we bag any of 'em, we'll send an amplifier."

Fiedler dropped down the hole.

The minutes dragged on into an hour . . . and then, finally, the voice of the exec growled up through the hole:

"You can pull the plug any time now—you're set!"

Connaway glanced at the four-striper, noted no disapproval and yelled, *"Clear the bridge! Dive! Dive!"*

Sculpin went to periscope depth a few seconds after her bridge officers scrambled down the hole. At sixty-three feet, Connaway wrapped his arms around the handles of *Sculpin's* high scope and quickly focused the lens. Then his voice gushed tersely in the darkened cubicle.

"Masts coming down the track. Narrow bow angle. I can't make 'em out clearly from here, but they look like freighters with a can escort . . ."

On the sound gear, RM 3/c Charles Taylor suddenly twisted around and growled softly:

"Fast screws, Captain! Bearing two two five, sir!"

Connaway swung the periscope sharply. The can was coming down the track. *Well,* he thought, *if the bastard's in the mood for a down-the-throat shot I'll oblige!* Connaway grunted the order to open the outer torpedo doors forward. A dull *thump* reverberated through the boat in response. Then Connaway, face plastered to the 'scope, snarled the order to stand by with three fish.

"Range three thousand yards—how does it look on the TDC?"

"Green light, Captain! Keep on lining him!" came the reply.

Taylor grunted: "He's coming faster, Captain!"

"Angle on the bow five, range two five seven oh —stand by to shoot 'em off at two thousand yards exactly!"

"How's the convoy?" Cromwell growled.

"Same as before, Captain. Still coming . . . wait! *They're changing course up there—they're beginning to turn left!*"

"Turn with 'em!" the division commander snapped.

"How's the setup on the can?"

"Good!" the TDC yelled up.

"Left five degrees—standby *Fire one! Fire two! Fire three!* Left full rudder—*take her down deep!*"

Connaway pried his arms off the periscope and stared down at the stopwatch ticking away in Cromwell's hand. On the sound gear, Taylor was checking the audible run. *Nothing.* Then a long five minutes later, as submariners forgot their intense disappointment and braced themselves for a string of Jap ash cans, the end run of three torpedoes boomed harmlessly on the bottom. But the can had darted away safely at the last second, having spotted the triple wake of *Sculpin's* torpedoes.

"What's with that Jap?" Cromwell snapped. "Turn that receiver on audio, sailor—"

Taylor complied. The convoy, moving emergency left, was hightailing it in the same tight formation as originally. But the can had simply moved over their spot and, after a few desultory swings to pick up a sound contact, was moving off too! Cromwell and Connaway masked their intense gloom in a hasty conference, the result of which was to stay put for about an hour and then run like hell on another end-around.

But again no contact report was transmitted. Precious minutes passed in a desperate bid to get into firing position ahead of the convoy. Finally, just before dawn, Connaway cleared the bridge and pulled the plug. Minutes later, at periscope depth again, he began calling down observations to the TDC operator by way of a J-1 talker at his elbow.

"Range, 6,500 yards—and coming!" he whispered tersely. "Five ships. Destroyer apparently in rear. Zig-zagging along base course. Open outer doors forward!"

The command was academic at this point. In the forward torpedo room, doors were open and a CPO was standing by, ready to fire manually if the electric firing system cut out. Throughout the silent compartments, all hands intoned fervent prayers for slightly more than the successful pickling of Jap ships. There were prayers for their own safety, and the prayers were fully warranted: once warned, Jap merchantmen would disperse instantly upon detection of an enemy sub in their immediate area.

Or so it said in the book.

Connaway, draped around the periscope and sweating profusely, snarled continuous ranges, bow angles and torpedo setting data. Beside him, stopwatch in hand, was Cromwell. From the forward room came the telephoned word that six fish were set for small gyro angle, depth twelve feet, generated run 1,800 yards.

"You can fire in one minute!" snapped the J-1 talker, repeating the word from control. "All lights green in TDC."

"This is what we came for," Cromwell intoned softly. "Get 'em right, Fred."

Nobody spoke. Nobody breathed.

The sweet second hand moved inexorably around sixty endless seconds and then the man at the periscope snapped: *Fire one! Fire two! Fire three! Fire four! Fire five! Fire six!* Left full rud—"

But there the command broke off. Connaway, flattened to the peepsight, suddenly howled:

"Take 'er down deep—fast! Take 'er down!"

Connaway swiveled around to the four-striper, his face ashen.

"They saw something, Captain. They turned toward us to ram!"

On the sound gear, Taylor reported screws closing at fifteen knots and passing overhead. In the background, he said, a destroyer was coming down the track with a bone in her teeth.

Below, in the control room, the diving officer watched the depth gauge move around to 100 . . . 125 . . . 175 feet. Then Taylor was hearing that destroyer passing up the flank of the merchantman. Cromwell put the stopwatch aside, looked at his young boat skipper and said:

"Hold onto your hat, son. Here they come."

And they came. First the merchantmen slowly thrashed overhead, a sound that was audible even at *Sculpin's* depth. Then the can moved through the slower, mushier sound and moved from the quarter to the bow, spinning into a tight circle.

"Shut off all machinery! Rig for depth charge!" Connaway whispered. "Take 'er down to 250 and sit there—"

As the submarine plunged at a 15 degree dive angle, the first of the Jap depth charges rained down —fourteen of them in a broken string that shattered light bulbs, spilled charts and generally gave Connaway's fleet boat a light working over. The worst effect, however, was above the diving platform where Lieutenant Joe Defrees was standing. Here the depth gauge suddenly and inexplicably stuck at 210 feet. Defrees whirled around to the J-1 in control:

"Tell the captain that depth isn't recording—the needle shot down to 125 feet and is stuck there!"

Connaway looked at his boss when the word flashed up.

"Send the battle surface crew to the tower!" he snapped. "Tell the diving officer to try and keep her on an even bubble—"

Sailors spilled onto the tower ladder seconds later as more alarming reports emanated from control.

Men in helmets and lifebelts—sweating, half-dressed men—gathered grimly in the tiny compartment listening to the low, terse voice of Taylor reporting the condition of the can. The crew sat silently for fifteen minutes—an endless wait. Word finally came.

"He's moving to the right, sir—*he's moving off, sir!*"

But without a depth gauge, *Sculpin* was helpless. Only after she'd popped to the surface with her battle surface crew racing to the deck guns did work start on the gauge repair. Cromwell, Connaway, Brown and four lookouts stared across the horizon at the tiny speck that was the Jap can moving away from them. If the Jap turned and charged back, there was no saving her as long as the depth gauge didn't register. There was no holding her down at an estimated depth and an estimated bubble. Below, it was a frantic race to repair, while on the bridge men with faces plastered to glasses watched in grim silence the disappearing speck. All guns were manned—the deck 5-inch, 20 and 40-mm. forward.

The sea was laved in bright sunshine, although none of it was to shine on Connaway's boat this day...

Suddenly, the frantic cry of the lookout forward broke the awful silence blanketing the bridge:

"Captain Connaway! That speck's growin'!"

Moments later, they could all make out the outlines of the enlarging ship. Connaway whirled around to the white-faced talker standing on the ladder.

"*How much longer?*" he roared. "*Ask Mister Defrees how much longer?*"

From the control room where the depth gauge lay dismantled, came a desperate grunt: "You'll have to hold the bastards off a while, Captain. We can't get this thing fixed for another five minutes at least!"

The speck loomed larger, white water pushing

ahead as it obviously sheered off to the starboard to bring all guns to bear.

"Commence fire!" Connaway leaned over the fair-water at the 40-mm. mount. Back on the cigarette deck at the after end of the tower, Brown was repeating the order to the 5-inch crew. Now a stuttering cacophony of tracers and puffballs roared out from the two gun mounts as *Sculpin*, licking her wounds like an injured tiger, flailed away at the enemy destroyer. Giant plumes of bracketing fire mushroomed up around the onrushing, as yet silent can.

A minute later, all Jap broadsides roared out and tracers arced across the shortening distance. Fountains of red-stained water leaped up around the rolling submarine, conned in these moments by John Cromwell. Then Defrees raced up the ladder and relieved Cromwell, passing the word that it was *impossible* to repair the gauge after all. Cromwell went below to the diving stand for a look with his own eyes.

"Get me a high pressure line!" Cromwell bawled. "Someone hand me that oil squirt. There must be a w—"

John Cromwell never finished the sentence.

Topside, three men standing below the periscope shears suddenly slammed deckward in a bloody heap, as a Jap shell ripped through the bridge and another through the main induction. Screams and frantic shouting and gunfire echoed downward; bodies tumbled down the tower ladder and then a strong voice was heard calling from the bridge:

"Commander Connaway's been killed!"

A second later: "They're closing fast—everybody topside's dead!"

The announcer was Brown, who just missed the shells because he'd walked back to say something to the 5-inch gun captain. Two of the four lookouts were dead, too, he screamed.

And in this precise moment, the four-striper knew his fate.

"Mister Brown," he calmly directed the battle-shocked junior officer, "You will please go forward and check the boat. *Now!*"

Cromwell swiveled left and watched the cascade of blood-soaked men tumbling from the conning tower ladder. They were still coming as the staccato chattering of Jap 20's reverberated wildly along the superstructure. Chief of the Boat Gabrunas, assisting the wounded men through the induction, howled down that the induction was jammed and holed.

Cromwell sucked in his breath and looked around slowly at the grim-faced, battered crew congregated in the control room.

"Okay," he said softly. "Pass the word to open the vents—everybody topside. This fight is over . . ."

Jap hardware was thundering aboard the submarine for fair, perforating her bridge, tearing up her decks, holing her shears, bending back proud steel like matchpaper. Crewmen raced to the fore and aft escape hatches in a desperate bid to haul clear, before *Sculpin* admitted the sea.

But in the wardroom, young Ensign Max Fiedler calmly sat sipping a cup of black coffee. As frantic crewmen raced up the companionway to the torpedo escape hatch, Fiedler reached for a pinochle deck and began shuffling himself a last hand. Somebody shouted that the boat was going down fast, yet the ensign remained seated, and with a curious air of detachment, dealt the cards of Death.

About ten men chose to go down with *Sculpin* for reasons that nobody will ever know. *In extremis*, there is no accounting for human behavior, or why a man will willingly sacrifice his life. Certainly only John Cromwell—now slouched silently against the rail of the diving stand, head bowed, staring vacantly at the fast-filling compartment—had sufficient reason to forfeit his life. He'd taken the calculated risk and lost, and to his way of reasoning there was no alternative to Death.

As the water rose to *Sculpin's* decks and then to the base of her bridge, crewmen hurled themselves overboard into the bright, brassy sea, striking out hard to swim free of the dying sub's pull. Few could bear to look back, but one or two who did remarked that the sub went down "on an even keel" as an "all vents open situation" would logically dictate.

IJN *Yokahama*, a sleek Fubuki-class destroyer closed with guns no longer blazing. On her decks stood many sailors with heaving lines and lifejackets. As the can closed the little knots of misery in the oily water, her diesels stopped and several white-clad officers appeared on her bridge. Then the lifejackets and heaving lines sailed over, and the survivors struggled to gain *Yokahama's* decks.

W. H. Welsh S 1/c, wounded in the arm and eye, was immediately thrown overboard by a Jap CPO. Then the shocked survivors were bulled into two ranks and made to stand at attention as the Jap commanding officer came down for inspection. J. P. Rourke GM 3/c, injured internally, desperately fought three enemy swabbies who grabbed him, but the destroyer CO intervened at the last moment. They were wounded, bloody, oil-soaked men and their submarine was gone—that, curiously, was enough for the Jap.

Ordering *Yokahama* back around on her base course and all prisoners herded below, the destroyer charged back to her convoy. For the duration of the war, *Sculpin's* survivors lived out their days in the Ashio copper mines, where submarine prisoners were usually taken.

Only a handful of men were ever repatriated at war's end, and, without variation, they told the story of *Sculpin's* finest hour. Captain John Cromwell, Subdiv 43, received the Congressional Medal of

Honor posthumously for sacrificing his life for his country; posthumously, Commander Fred Connaway was awarded the Silver Star.

Sculpin, gone to glory, became a legend in death.

HELL PATROL

"CAPTAIN to the bridge!"

The command crackled twice over the sub's intercom. Instantly, a spate of pounding footsteps echoed up through the control room. Lieutenant Jim Nickerson, draped tensely around the handles of USS *Bergall's* high periscope, was squinting at distant, fading masts. It was dusk, 1800, December 13, 1943.

The submarine—on station in the South China Sea and making preparations for a mine plant—was nine days out of Fremantle, Australia, on her second war patrol. CRM John MacKay, the radarman, homed in for range, speed and course of the enemy contact.

Tall, taut-muscled Commander John M. Hyde swung up the control room ladder. Lieutenant Nickerson relinquished the periscope to his skipper.

"Masts, Captain. Hell of a way off," he said as Hyde took his first look. The masts evoked a tight grin.

"Nice work, Jim. Radar—what've you got?"

"Couple of blurs, Captain," Mackay reported as he fiddled with the focus dial. A second later his voice rose sharply. "Correction, sir—*two* targets definitely!"

The exec, Lieutenant Robert Ison, climbed into

the tower and took the periscope. Behind him came
Lieutenant Commander Ben Jarvis, riding the
Seventh Fleet boat as a guest observer. The six-four,
230-pound former Annapolis linesman tapped Ison
impatiently.

"Man, don't hog it!"

"Range: 35,000. Speed: 14 knots. Course: 055
True, Captain!" MacKay snapped.

"General quarters. Night torpedo attack," the CO
ordered. To Lieutenant Nickerson he said, "Take
over again, Jim. Sing out if anything happens—"

Ordering up flank speed on four mains as the
alarm went grating through the sub, Commander
Hyde climbed up to the bridge. Ensign Edward Welch
was searching along the line of bearing, but neither
Welch nor the five sailors clinging to the shears saw
the targets. The submarine lunged through the calm
sea at 20 knots, cutting a creamy-white bow wave
and tossing back a fine chill spray.

"Any idea what they are, Captain?" Ensign Welch
inquired.

"Nope. Could be tankers, Mister," the captain
said impassively. "Could be just about anything at
this range."

Ensign Welch said admiringly, "That Nickerson's
got some pair of eyes!"

"So's the high scope. Gives us fifty feet elevation
over the surface, Mister."

Ison and Jarvis joined them. A surge of excitement coursed all compartments, for the sighting of
contacts actually changed their mission from the dull
and prosaic business of planting mines to the contact
and destruction of major Japanese shipping.

At flank speed, the exec computed, it would be
another couple of hours before *Bergall* would identify
targets. The use of the high periscope was risky: it
exposed the sub to detection but, paradoxically, increased its chances of spotting and identifying the
contacts because the radar beam, at fifty feet above

the surface, or normal surface lookout, had a proportionately greater range to sweep.

It was almost dark now. Hyde, Ison and Jarvis went below to the plotting boards, and after another few minutes Hyde snapped on the intercom:

"This is the captain. We have targets twenty miles distant and are making an end-around for night torpedo attack. That is all."

On disseminating information to a sub crew, there were two schools of thought: Never say anything because it put men on a fine edge [anyway, targets had a way of vaporizing at times]; and tell the crew everything—it invests them with the proper *esprit*. John Hyde believed in the latter. He had eight previous patrols to his record, and the best ones were invariably those which shared the excitement of the chase.

At 1900 MacKay reported again: "Targets steady, Captain. They look like a couple of moving islands—"

The report was delivered to Hyde in the wardroom. There was time for coffee and a smoke. Hyde, Ison and Jarvis were huddled over the charts of Royalist Bank.

"Eleven to fourteen fathoms, Captain," Ison said softly, tapping the point of expected attack. "We either get both ships or we'll end up slugging it out on top."

"Maybe it's not so bad as we think," Hyde shrugged. "Maybe they're only tankers."

"You're whistling in a graveyard." Jarvis glanced over his pipe. "Them pips keep gettin' bigger all the time."

"Calculated risk," the CO said with finality. He drained his cup, took a refill and slipped into his parka. "If we can't submerge, Ben this sub's got a damn good gun crew."

"I hope so," big Jarvis grimaced. "The footnotes claim there's rocks like cathedrals forty feet under."

"Captain! This is maneuvering room... We're going to have to cut back to standard speed. Too much vibration!"

Hyde snapped the intercom talkback: "Go ahead. Let me know our maximum speed."

"Walk. Don't run to nearest enemy targets," Ison winced. "Well, anything's preferable to mine laying."

The wardroom parlay broke up on a cheerless note as Commander Richard Bryan stuck his head in the door.

"Captain, we're making eighteen knots. That's absolute maximum unless you want to shake a strut loose."

"In emergency, Bryan," Hyde pressed, "couldn't we squeeze out a few extra turns?"

"Don't bet on it, sir." The motor mac mopped his face. "We're just liable to end up sitting ducks."

Hyde nodded glumly. The three officers adjourned to the control room. The maneuvering board had two targets now bearing 102 True at 26,000 yards. Aside from the loss of speed, *Bergall* was functioning smoothly. Hyde climbed into the conning tower at 1920 hours.

"Big fat bastards," the radarman grunted. "When do you think we'll spot 'em, Captain?"

"Half hour or so. Keep your eyes on that scope, MacKay, and keep those bearings coming!"

The night was clear and the sea calm. No stars. Only Venus lighted the South China Sea to the horizon. Nine men, including the lookouts, filled the confined bridge. All talk was muffled, sporadic, tense in an understated way. The decision to make like a PT was John Hyde's and the knowledge that he could hit and run but couldn't dive in the rock-strewn water drove a queaziness to the pit of his flat stomach.

Hyde was thirty-four, a lean, gray-eyed six footer. SS 320, the *Bergall*, was his world—the same world that spawned the likes of such heroic sub skippers as Howard Gilmore, Sam Dealy and John Cromwell. It was a world in which a man and his boat were one and the same. Through the identity of his submarine, so did he have an identity.

Below, in the cubicle of a captain's cabin was a framed picture' of his wife and infant son. Hyde thought across six thousand miles of Pacific until the vibrations of his other wife claimed his undivided attention. Forcing *Bergall* into an action whereby she couldn't dive, couldn't run full gait, seemed an act of disloyalty in a way. Grimly, Hyde turned to the giant beside him.

"See anything, Ben?"

"Yeah. Too much light," Jarvis said acidly, nodding at Venus. "Maybe the Nips got good lookouts tonight, too—"

The skipper brought up his glasses and scanned the dark horizon, knowing the enemy targets were still beyond range. The strain told on all of them now. He stared up at the five lookouts hanging in the shears, night glasses plastered to their intense faces.

"Captain, gun crews standing by."

Bob Ison was standing on the conning tower ladder, only the top half of him on the bridge. Hyde acknowledged.

"What's the range to targets, Bob?"

"Twenty-two thousand yards, Captain."

"How does it look on the board?"

"*Hot*. They're good size blips, John," the exec smiled boyishly. "You know something? Today's the thirteenth."

"I thought of it," Hyde grinned, foolishly.

So did the rest of *Bergall's* crew. The number had a pleasant connotation aboard the sub. On the thirteenth of May her keel was laid; 13 months later to the day Hyde assumed command; the boat was launched on February 13 and arrived at Pearl Harbor for assignment on August 13. On October 13, a 4,500-ton tanker and two escorts stood out from Camranh Bay across *Bergall's* track. *Three* torpedoes put her down; only *ten* depth charges were dropped.

Bergall's first patrol was climaxed with the killing of a seventeen thousand ton tanker and a smaller fleet oiler. From start to finish the attack lasted 13 minutes.

The range to targets closed steadily. At 1920 Ben Jarvis leaned on the gunshield and kept his glasses fixed at 105 True. Range was down to 19,500 yards. He jabbed the commanding officer.

"See 'em, Captain! Two points on the starboard bow!"

It was only a fraction of a second later that the lookouts in the shears made the same sighting. The targets were tiny blotches on a stark horizon, but getting larger and not zigging suddenly. Quickly, Hyde dropped his glasses and lowered himself through the conning tower into the control room. The tracking party took over, Ison working on the bearings for TDC.

The sub was lunging ahead for an end-around, trying to keep ahead but unobserved by the enemy ships. A few minutes later:

"Range: 12,000 yards, Captain."

"Battle stations."

The gonging was superfluous. Most of *Bergall's* crew were already stationed. Hyde secured the gun crew and clambered up the conning tower ladder to topside. He stood beside Ben Jarvis, who had incredible night vision.

"Looks like a heavy cruiser and an escort," Jarvis said slowly. "Escort is barely visible ahead of her."

"Ask radar where the escort is," Hyde grunted at the bridge radioman. Over the intercom, the answer was shot back: "Two thousand yards ahead starboard beam of the target."

"That puts us on his port beam," Hyde commented.

"Target is zigzagging. Target is increasing speed, sir!" the bridge radioman repeated radar's information. "Course: Zero three five, sir."

"Very well."

Inexorably, the tension mounted. Throughout the sub, men whispered that they were taking on a heavy cruiser and probably a light. Lieutenant Ison went topside, and in his efforts to identify the target, stayed long enough to see turrets plainly. The primary target was reassessed as a Tone or Atago Class light cruiser. Both vessels were still overlapping from the angle of chase. The time was 2030; range 6,000 yards. Radar suddenly reported interference.

"Make ready all tubes. Stand by to fire."

Hyde was on the TBT binoculars. The submarine was moving up fast on both targets. A steady succession of radar bearings surged up to the bridge. Torpedoes were set for fourteen feet; a full nest of six was ready. Outer doors were open. The radar interference intensified as *Bergall* bore in, firing range predicted for 3,000 yards. John Hyde's hard stomach danced a tango as he worried about the fish soon to be underway in a glassy sea.

"Captain! They're signaling with blinker lights!"

"Give me a range—quick!"

"Range three seven double oh," radar came back.

"Range three six double oh, Captain."

Only the voice of the talker cut the stifling silence on *Bergall's* bridge. Hyde felt cold sweat spanking through his shirt.

"Stand by forward!"

"Final setup!"

"Bearing—mark!"

"Set!" From the TDC man.

Bergall had swung a full 90 degrees and was boring in, range 3,500 yards. The targets filled Hyde's glasses—damned big and damned plainly silhouetted.

"Fire one! Fire two! Fire three! Fire four! Fire five! Fire six!"

A spread of accurately spaced tinfish leaped out in a widening fan at the targets. Both vessels were now signalling frantically as Hyde ordered left full rudder, all ahead full! *Bergall* got out of her track. Six phosphorescent streaks tore up the dwindling gulf between submarine and target. Nobody spoke. Ison had the stop watch. Jarvis jabbed Hyde as the full outline of the "escort" suddenly became recognizable as another cruiser!

Time ticked off inexorably... Ten seconds... twenty... thirty... forty...

"Ought to be hitting about now, Ca—"

Two explosions shot flames eight hundred feet in the air, enveloping the target simultaneously. The concussive roar belched a hot blast of fiery fragments across the sea and changed night to brightest day. Between the monumental flames the men on the submarine's bridge saw what was left of a heavy cruiser [*Myoko*] as she tore apart, disgorging men and steel into an indifferent sea. Shock after shock rattled the submarine, smothering sounds of jubilation under the incalculable thunder of exploding magazines. The bridge radioman yelled *"Three blips, Captain! Radar's got three Japs sitting out there now!"*

Hyde blinked at the holocaust, then wheeled around and dropped into the conning tower. Over the bedlam MacKay was saying:

"We busted 'er in half, Captain!"

"Good but not good enough."

When he got to the bridge the two fires were distinct. The shattered bridge structure loomed up like a sick whale; the stern section was down angled and pathetic; waving figures were leaping into spreading oil fires. The second cruiser came abeam of the forward section, then stopped dead. No attempt to punish by gunfire followed the fleeing raider. Hyde was intrigued.

The logical time for a submarine in shoal waters to run like hell was now, but Hyde decided to run in the *opposite* direction. The tantalizing spectacle of an intact Japanese cruiser framed in the garish flames evoked inevitable orders:

"Forward room. Make ready a reload!"

Ison nudged the CO. "He's got a pickle [torpedo] in him sure as God made little apples, Skipper! He was 2,000 yards on the far side, but on the straight and narrow with our fish. We hit him an overlapping shot—"

"I believe it, John." Jarvis clapped Hyde's back like an affectionate bear. "You pickled both of 'em."

At 2100 hours, range was 9,300 yards. Speed was reduced to allow for the reload. Slowly, malevolently, *Bergall* came about on her heading for the second ship. The escape clause was gone, irretrievably dismissed. The *raison d'etre* of a submarine was the destruction of enemy shipping, not running in a manner that left doubts in the minds of her men.

The bridge radioman chirped: "Forward room reports all tubes ready, sir."

"Stand by. Bearing—*mark!*" He looked up from the TBT. "We'll fire a spread of six at two five double-oh!"

"My God, Captain!" Jarvis exploded. "They're shooting at us!"

Twin flashes appeared forward of the escort.

"Salvo of two, Captain!" a lookout yelled.

Hyde jumped away from the TBT.

"Left full rudder—all ahead flank!"

The submarine heeled like a frightened colt as the first shells screamed a pair of fireballs straight at her. The first shell exploded in her wake, close aboard the stern, the second flashing over the bridge. Geysers of water drenched the quivering deck as Hyde bellowed for right full rudder. The second salvo was closer, and although the range was great—9,000 yards—*Bergall* was in the bag for Japanese gunners.

Forward, a flash of light fused with the whimper of rending steel. A sheet of flame mushroomed up from the torpedo loading hatch. Direct hit! *Bergall* shuddered but her speed held constant. Hyde felt sick to his stomach.

"Come about! Full ahead!" the CO snarled. "Damage control to the forward room—"

The third salvo screamed in, punching up twin mountains of China Sea through which the sub gratefully raced. A cascade of water deluged her decks, smothering the flame. Hyde's voice was suddenly calm. The third salvo ended it.

"Secure outer doors. Secure from torpedo attack. Lieutenant Nickerson, get your gun crews topside on the double."

Time: 2106. An open intercom from the forward torpedo room telegraphed the awesome sound of coughing, cursing men and the sputtering of an electrical fire. Then the voice of Warrant Electrician Smith, of the damage control party, grated through the miasma.

"We got it, Captain! Fire in the forward room!"

Hyde started down the hole. "Jarvis—take over. Put distance between us and those bastards!"

He ran through the submarine, pushing his way through the millrace of dazed, bloody sailors emerging from the stricken compartment. Inside, port side, a half dozen desperate sailors were attempting to smother a fire behind the sound gear; smaller fires directly under the hatch and along the overhead were being attacked by mattresses. Hyde grabbed Lieutenant Harold Drew, DCO. Smitty was unshackling the sound gear and needed a hand.

"We can handle it, Captain."

"Okay. Get as much gear out of this compartment as possible. I'm going to seal it off."

Smitty yelled, "All the mattresses you can bring forward, Captain—*fast!*"

Like ugly snakes, running electrical fires were sparking out along the whole length of the forward room. Damage control took over and Hyde went through the wardroom. His orders to the chief of the boat were clipped, concise, specific:

"Get on the ball. Masks. Mattresses. Send Doc forward."

Chief Torpedoman Cost emerged from the smoke-filled compartment and caught up to the CO. His report was thorough, accurate:

"Projectile entered after port side of the room, Captain. Pressure hull got it aft of Frame 35. The hatch is finished and the hull's grooved from outboard on the starboard side. The JP tripod's finished and so's the high salvage connection. Starboard riser got it at the Number one main ballast tank."

"In other words?"

"We damn well better not dive, sir."

"Okay."

Hyde started into the radio shack. The pharmacist's mate emerged from the galley and caught him.

"Shock and burns. That's all, Captain."

"Okay. Do your job, Doc."

Cost swiveled around.

"That shell hole, Captain. It was an eight-incher."

Hyde scribbled a message and found the communicator standing at his elbow. "Code it and get it off fast."

The message was the action report to ComSubs Seventh Fleet and gaunt, game John Hyde felt miserable as he spelled it out. He went forward again. The forward room bulkhead flapper was off now, but Vodopich, Bryant, Ott and Wilson were on top of the worst of it. The smoked-smudged features of young Harold Wilson broke into a valiant grin as the CO reentered the compartment.

"Captain, we still kicked the living hell out of 'em tonight ..."

Commander Hyde went topside and stood beside the forlorn giant, Ben Jarvis. The message was sent on a course that would indicate to the Japs that *Bergall* was heading toward Brunei Bay. For what it was worth, it appeared to be a worthy ruse. Jarvis thought so. On the horizon now was only one fire and smoke, a gray curtain blanketing the area.

Ahead lay 2,200 miles of open sea for a submarine no longer able to submerge.

Ahead lay mined, heavily patrolled Karimata Strait, across the length of Java Sea to Lombok Strait. All it took was the sighting by one Japanese plane and the silver-winged squadrons could bomb her at their leisure. The unbearable conglomeration of thoughts pinpointed almost certain destruction of *Bergall*, yet at the same time it heightened gray-eyed John Hyde's resolve to bring her in safely. The night was still clear, still perfect for a Jap squadron to come roaring over for vengeance.

All guns fore and aft were manned.

All hands were acutely aware of their desperate, almost hopeless plight. Few slept. Gunners took rotation at the coffee urn, condemning the Japs with faint bravado. Coffee was sent to the bridge in buckets, but neither Jarvis nor Hyde needed a stimulus. No radar interrupted the prayers with sudden contacts, but a constant succession of damage control reports shuttled up to the bridge. Hyde secured GQ, yet all guns were manned.

The score was a heavy cruiser halved and unquestionably sunk, and probably a seriously wounded light cruiser. It was consolation as morning welled up out of the sea—bright, too clear and hellishly calm. At 0600, over Jarvis's objections, Hyde ordered his junior officer below to sleep.

"Don't argue. I need you to spell me, Ben. Ison's got all he can handle with damage control," Hyde growled into his coffee. "Shove off before I bawl in this brew."

"Stop blaming yourself."

"I'm not. This is my boat. I just feel miserable."

"Okay. Sing out. I'll be flaked out in the control room."

Hyde started to say get in a bunk, but Jarvis smiled at him and dropped through the hole [conning tower]. He found a place and curled up like a bear that resents hibernation.

On deck, in all compartments, the coming of day was a time for making peace with one's God and one's shipmate. The Filipino mess attendant shambled back from officers' country to the radio shack. He calmly put two hundred crisp two dollar bills on the desk.

"Here, Joe. Remember that big game in Pearl? Well, the deck was fishy."

In the control room the man on the six-hundred-pound manifold unburdened himself as an electrician passed him.

"You lost a train ticket last year. We were both chasing the same dame. I knew you were busted but I swiped the ticket anyway. Go ahead and clip me."

"Some other time. I gotta tell Smitty what happened to his car the night some sonuvabitch swiped it . . ."

Time dragged: 1155. Nothing on the intercom. It was inconceivable to think the Japs had suddenly stopped flying their milk runs from Soerabaja to Balikpapan. And yet . . . why not? Radarman MacKay fought to discipline his mind as his eyes were disciplined. He watched with somber intensity the arm sweeping over a black screen. Nobody smoked in the tower, but it was different this morning. Anything was okay with the old man now. He had a bottle of twelve-year-old cognac in his locker and the idea of wallowing in liquor brought the taste a-nagging. He pulled a cigarette but it hung slack in his open jaws. The yellow blip came onto the screen!

"Aircraft! Bearing: One zero six degrees! Distance twelve miles!"

Simultaneously, topside, the JOD [junior officer of the deck] yelled:

"There! Enemy aircraft, Captain! ... There!"

"Hold your fire! Hold your fire!" Hyde boomed.

The submarine rared into life, determined to sell that life dearly. Guns were trained on target, following it. All stations were manned and ready in thirty seconds. The plane was a float-type snooper. Standard observation bomber. It was large to begin with and got increasingly larger as eighty-four sailors said their prayers. Commander Hyde gripped the spray shield beside Ben Jarvis. The plane—a Mavis —swung down the starboard beam, not circling, not dipping toward the water.

For a full minute nobody spoke. The radar opened out the range. Finally Jarvis grinned weakly. On deck, sailors blinked at one another in utter disbelief.

"She sight us, John?"

"If she did, then why didn't she drop one?"

"Maybe she's riding light."

"Then you can expect Zeroes. She'll hang off there and yell for help."

"Maybe God," Jarvis licked his lips, "made the bastards blind."

There was no other explanation, unless prayers by the bucketful were suddenly acknowledged. The devout and the irreligious were one, for the Mavis didn't return. GQ secured. The regular deck gun watch took over. Commander Hyde sank to his deck and dropped his cap over his eyes as a sunshield. It covered a multitude of silent tears.

Eight hours later, Commander John Hyde dispatched his first amplifying report to Commander Seventh Fleet. Hell broke loose in Perth as Hyde anticipated it might. Until then, all that was known at submarine headquarters was that *Bergall* had

battled a couple of Jap giants off Royalist Bank and
busted one good.

Reaction was swift from Admiral Ralph W. Christie: *Bergall* was ordered to head north, in the opposite direction, to North Natuna; there, three subs
would make a rendezvous with *Bergall*, and Hyde
was ordered to scuttle her in deep water.

Hyde read the message several times in the shack.
The responsibility was solely his for the ship, for
the crew. A storm the likes of which could mean his
naval career might descent from disregarding Admiral Christie's orders. But it was the chance he
had to take.

"No reply, Sparks."

"Nothing?" The CRM looked up quizzically

"That's right. Nothing."

The thing was on his conscience, strictly his. Jarvis, none of his regular officers, fought him. Throughout the boat, men spoke in fierce defense of a captain who could defy Admiral Christie. It was a long
night. Radio messages to subs in the vicinity of
Northern Natuna sputtered out from CTF 71. After
midnight of the fifteenth, the gaunt, gray-eyed submariner allowed himself the luxury of slumping over
his coffee cup in the wardroom. No contacts. Weather mugging up. It wasn't much to pin a miracle on.

The next morning at 1100, periscope lookout
picked up an American sub traveling at high speed
surfaced. She was *USS Angler* under Commander
Howard Bissel, speeding to make the Natuna rendezvous. Recognition was swift, the boats closed and
Bissel bellowed through a megaphone:

"Man, the whole fleet's looking for you—turn
around. You've got orders to scuttle!"

"How was the passage through Lombok?"

"Planes. Lousy with planes. *Why?*"

"That's where we're headed, Howie." Hyde could
see the exchange of looks on *Angler's* bridge. He said,
"I hate to foul up your patrol, but I'll have to ask

you to take part of my crew aboard. I'm taking this boat all the way to the barn."

The incredulous Bissel stared at the battered sub for a long moment, but he didn't argue the point.

"How many men do you want to put aboard?"

"Fifty-four. Fifty-five."

"You'll never make it."

Hyde shrugged. "There's deep water near the barn. If I've got to scuttle, I'd just as soon do it closer to home."

The captain of the *Angler* nodded mutely and with compassionate affection. He sheared away from the battered *Bergall* and found deep water. Rendezvous time was 1930 that night.

"This is the captain speaking," Hyde opened the hardest speech he ever made. "Fifty-four men and one officer will be transferred to *Angler* tonight. I'm sorry to have to separate a wonderful crew, but the risk is too great ... odds overwhelmingly against survival of this submarine. If your name is called, go and don't argue. There's no appealing this order ... God bless you. May we meet again ..."

The arguments about who stays, who goes continued up to the time of the rendezvous. *Angler* surfaced on schedule and hove to alongside. The transfer was swift, painful, but completed without interruption.

Then eight officers and twenty enlisted men began the hardest part of the voyage. Hyde said little, slept less. He took the deck of his heroic submarine as she entered the mined, heavily patrolled passage of Lombok. He refused to relinquish the deck until the submarine had passed safely into the Indian Ocean. Then, for the first time in five nights, Hyde allowed Jarvis to help him down from the bridge and put him in his bunk for a night's sleep.

Southwest gales shrouded the incredible passage on the last day. Hyde, smelling land, sent a message to CTF 71, advising Admiral Christie that *Bergall* was south of the barrier. That afternoon Hyde sailed her down to Exmouth Gulf where welders patched on temporary plates over the pressure hull. Repairs effected in a few hours, *Bergall* started out for Fremantle and one of the most fantastic welcomes ever given a returning submarine.

The voyage ended at 0900 December 23 when Admiral Christie came aboard and unorthodoxly hugged the unshaven gray-eyed submariner till it hurt. When *Angler* brought the rest of the crew in, there wasn't a dry eye in the house or a sober soul in the Navy Yard.

Post-war records, based on unverified sinkings, do not allow for halving an enemy cruiser. *Bergall* sank only the stern half of *Myoko*. The bow survived, in itself a miracle. The Japanese towed it to a Naval shipyard, and there it rusted until the Japanese surrender.

Commander John Hyde was awarded the Navy Cross for extraordinary heroism under fire. The vessel that he was ordered to scuttle received an extensive refit and was back on the firing line two months later for the completion of a distinguished service career in the submarine fleet.

THE KID ENSIGN
AND THE SUB-INVADING JAPS

THE NIGHT was moonless and squally. Standing JOD watch on the bridge of the submarine *Redfin,* Ensign Gene Helz and four other sailors, clinging to the periscope shears, gazed out over black water. Lightning flashes pierced the thunderheads over Balabac Strait.

It was 10 P.M. April 21, 1944. The *Redfin* was heading back to the barn after its second war patrol and three Jap ships torpedoed to hell. The four seamen were talking in low voices of the wild soirees with the Kobber girls coming up in Fremantle, but twenty-four-year-old Ensign Helz's mind was on business. Just to the north was Admiral Ozawa's Philippine Fleet. Over the horizon to the east was the Jap naval base of Tawi Tawi. The *Redfin* wasn't in Fremantle yet.

Lieutenant Commander C. K. Miller, the *Redfin's* executive officer, climbed the conning tower ladder and stood beside Helz. Finally he said, "Any business, Gene?"

"No, sir," he said formally, then grinned, "it's quiet, Rollo."

Miller nodded. They leaned against the spray shield watching the bow cut water in a wash of lum-

82

inescence. Then Miller said softly: "It won't be quiet for long, Gene. We just got a message."

"Sir?"

"Yes," Miller said. "From Comsouwespac in Fremantle. Six Australian commandos on Borneo between Dent Haven and Labuan. Lots of Japs there, and the Aussies want off. We're elected."

"When?"

"April 22. Any time after dark."

Helz said nothing for a moment, then: "There's a hell of a surf running."

"Always is."

"Who's going to go, Rollo?"

The exec shrugged.

"That," Miller said, "is what I came up here to talk to you about, Gene."

The JOD was silent. Above in the shears, an embarrassed sailor listened to the silence and coughed nervously. The submarine dipped fiercely into a dark sea and it rolled back high against her 40-mm mount, spraying the bridge. As the sea abated, Helz wiped his face.

"All right, Rollo," he said. "I'll go."

Miller said, "I told the captain I thought you would."

"How do we do it?"

"Rubber boat. We'll be just offshore, waiting."

"There's a hell of a current sweeps through there." Gene Helz looked at the exec. "I looked it up. Four knots."

"I know."

"When is this thing supposed to come off, sir?"

Miller shook his head. He studied the lean young ensign, then squeezed his shoulder affectionately.

"Captain's got the dope on that. Go down and talk to him," Miller said. "Oh, yeah! You'll need three men, Gene—"

"Well," he grinned, "at least I'll have company."

He turned the watch over to the exec, saluted and

started for the ladder. Rollo Miller turned with him.
The sub lunged under a heavier sea. Helz grabbed the
ladder and started down. In the faintness of light
reflected upward through the conning tower Helz
noted the exec's wince.

"One thing more, Gene! *Take single men.*"

Redfin's commanding officer, M.H. [Cy] Austin
was of the same opinion. Sitting in the wardroom
with Commander Austin, Ensign Helz wondered if
the ticking he felt in the pit of his stomach showed
on his face. If it did, Austin paid no attention. He
lunged through the briefing, pored over the coastal
charts and made tentative plans for the beach party.
So far as Gene Helz was concerned, the coffee was
the best part of it.

But the talk of machine guns, survival kits, et al,
was vaguely reassuring and after a while the ensign
excused himself and waded back through the submarine looking for three single men. He chose the
ship's yeoman, K. C. Harrington, a big, rangy ex-
Marine and crack marksman. Gunner's Mate Second G. E. Carrinder, the ordnance whiz, readily
volunteered. Finally Helz walked into the radio shack
and talked it over with RM 3/c R. E. Kahler, a
tough man in a brawl and an able communicator.

"There's time to change your minds," Gene Helz
told them collectively before he returned to the
bridge. "Sleep on it."

"Hell, Mister Helz!" Carrinder drawled as he lov-
ingly caressed a submachine gun. "Many times as I
handled this piece, I ain't never had a chance to pot
nothin'! I ain't interested in sleep, sir."

Feeling just about the same, the other volunteers
to *Redfin's* raid disdained the sack in the interests
of cloak-and-dagger. For them all it was, to be sure,
a somewhat unique experience in the business of war.
Hearing a torpedo *wrrang* against a steel hull was
not quite the same thing as making your own war,
though of course the satisfaction was there. What

fears or misgivings ran through their minds didn't
go into words. Instead, discussing the beach landing
and the contingencies that might arise, they formu-
lated a plan and at midnight they quit.

Gene Helz crawled in his sack forward and lay
there, quietly wondering what hell the six who'd
radioed were going through. In itself, the thought
was inspiring. He fell asleep. *Redfin* pawed her way
around the western tip of the island, a long, low
harbinger of death with an identity in the fleet. On
her first run, she'd neither seen nor fired at anything, but this bad memory was vindicated by a
triple strike the next time she went out. At the time,
three of anything in Japanese-controlled waters was
the stuff of which roaring good liberties are made.

Cy Austin's pickles ran straight, hot and true in
Palawan Passage. That ended the patrol and now
Redfin was on a line for Australia and a well-earned
liberty.

Cy Austin had filled Helz in on the background of
the Aussies waiting for a lift home. It was quite a
plague that Major F. Gorton Chester, British resi-
dent of North Borneo, had visited on the Japs occupying his home island. On October 6, 1943, *USS
Kingfisher* lifted "Gort" and five men from Western
Australia, sailing them to a swampy east coast shoal
off Labuan Point on Borneo. They set up shop immediately, checking on the movement of enemy
shipping along the north coast. Submarines *Tinosa*
in January 1944, and *Narwhal* in March 1944, rein-
forced the coast watchers and their polyglot army of
Chinese and Borneans. But at the start of April the
tide turned the other way; the Japs made the coast-
watching business a bloody one and it was reluctantly decided to abandon the north coast for a
healthier point of operation.

"Enter *Redfin*," Cy Austin told Helz in the wardroom. "You're not going in there with your head in

the clouds, boy. I want you to know that the deck is stacked to begin with."

"It's stacked worse against the Aussies, sir," the lanky Californian shrugged. "I'll get three good men. We'll try to bring 'em out."

Austin snapped, "That's all I ask, Gene! Give 'em a fair shake. They may be wounded or killed by now, for all Comsubs knows, so you search that beach real good. *Redfin* will be right behind you. You challenge with Victor. They'll send Victor back."

"If they're not there, Captain?"

"Then we'll take another stab at it."

"I'll do my best," the ensign said earnestly.

Austin grinned. "That's why Rollo went up to enlist you in the first place, kid. He figured on the basis of your lousy poker playing—you always go for inside straights."

"Yeah. I dote on 'em," Helz chuckled. "Sometimes I fill 'em, Captain."

"That's what the exec said, too."

When Helz awoke it was morning and the ship was motionless. *Redfin* was deep, lying submerged off North Borneo. Harrington, Carrinder and Kahler were fired by a sudden contagion of doubts. In the first place their paddles only numbered two pairs. Somebody had to make a couple, and the only available material was a deck-gunsight box and some one-inch pipe for handles.

"They ain't gonna do for this job, Guns," Harrington snorted. "They'll rip your hands off."

The rubber boat was inflated in the forward torpedo room two or three times with everybody in it. The regular watch standers sat around grinning at the routine. When the makeshift paddles came into play nobody could keep a straight face.

"*See?*" Yeoman Harrington snorted. "Ten gets you twenty they're not going to work out right."

Kahler cranked up his portable set.

"What the hell," growled Harrington, "are *you* doing?"

"Calling Jesus," the radioman replied. "He always does my heavy worrying."

"Put in a call for me," the ex-Marine groaned. And seeing Helz coming through the compartment door, the yeoman made it official. "Mister Helz. I got a feelin' we're goin' off half-cocked!"

"What's wrong?"

"We got a little paddle trouble here, it seems, sir."

"You can still change your mind, Yeo."

The sailor frowned.

"I'm *not* changing my mind, Mister Helz. I'm just makin' a point." He jumped out of the rubber boat. "Here! Get in, Mr. Helz—see for yourself."

"How's the gun and ammo department?" the radioman drawled. "We oughta take four Tommy guns, sir."

"Can't. There's only two." Gene Helz passed around cigarettes and the four of them sat in their boat smoking sullenly. "All right," the ensign said quietly after a minute. "Now that the bitching's all done, you fellas still with me?"

They said "yes" in unison. At 1100 they put away the boat and went to chow. At 1200 *Redfin* went to periscope depth and Austin gave the ensign his first look at North Borneo.

"That surf, sir," Helz muttered. "Does it ever lay down?"

"Slack water, it says in the book."

"That's about 2000." The ensign said thoughtfully. "I looked it up."

"The tide doesn't make for a couple of hours after that." The *Redfin's* captain took the scope back. "You'll have plenty of time on the beach, Gene."

The Californian felt warm sweat down the back of his khaki shirt. Austin hung on the periscope handles a while longer, then cranked them up and the sub went deep again. The two men walked forward to the wardroom and until 1400 studied the charts, such as they were, of the North Borneo coast. At 1500 Helz tried vainly to close his eyes, but the ticking started again. This beach, Austin's intelligence said, was lousy with Japs. They were poring over the British publications on North Borneo again when the speaker tube erupted:

"Captain! Fast screws bearing zero nine zero— coming in off the beach, sir!"

A moment later, at the forward torpedo room sound head, the sonarman wiped hot sweat from his headphones, passing them to Austin.

"Queer sounding sonuvagun, Captain."

Austin listened. The sonarman turned the dials left and right of the bearing. Then, centering back for a turn count, he mumbled:

"Could be *two* spitkits, Captain, huh?"

Commander Austin tossed the cans back at the sonarman and took off for the control room, Helz running a close second. The sub boiled to life. The screws were veering away now.

"Come to sixty-three feet! Keep 'er nice and steady, Rollo!"

The 'scope handles crept down and Cy Austin's long, hard frame warped grotesquely around the wet steel, swinging slowly around in a half circle.

"Sixty-three feet, sir!" the exec snapped.

There was silence in the control room, loud and long.

Then Austin snapped up the periscope handles and grunted:

"Ten. Take 'er down to ten feet, Rollo. I'd like to talk to Gene." Staring at the ensign, he said evenly, "You're not going to have a piece of cake, boy. They've got a crazy lugger and a steam launch running around off those swells. You look now. Up to sixty-three, Rollo!"

"Very well, sir."

Helz thought the lugger and the launch didn't look

as formidable as a *Fukuri* class DD, but this, he sensed, was simply false courage blowing up a storm. Austin dived the submarine again. Helz followed him to the wardroom where they checked what they saw against Japanese silhouettes.

"Don't check out." Cy Austin scratched his head. "It could be, boy, they're one of those local bums working with us. I say it because they're just off our projected position."

"Then that washes us out."

"Could be. Could well be," Austin mumbled. "We'll know something around sunset."

"I wonder what I'm going to tell those guys of mine." Helz said darkly. "You know, Captain, they're all built up to it now."

Austin gave him one of those looks. Discretion being the better response, the ensign excused himself and returned to the forward room. Disconsolately he stared at the quarter.

"You and your goddamn turn count!" he snorted at the sonar operator. Harrington, Carrinder and Kahler looked stunned. "We don't know whose boats they are—yet."

"Well," said the yeoman philosophically, "it's all in the cards. It was fun, wasn't it? We got a boat, we got all worked up—and lookit the stuff we collected!"

Assembled in a neat pile forward of the officers' head were flares [red and green], flashlight, four BARs and two Tommy guns.

Harrington bowed from the waist. "And, gentlemen, *How to Survive in the Jungle* in three volumes."

The man on the sound shrank three sizes. After a while he shrank a couple more because the "fast screws" went away. The four of them went to chow without much noise. At 1822 *Redfin* surfaced. It was shortly before sunset. The signalman of the watch cut loose a fast string of Victors. Instantly, from the rendezvous point, a series of three-dots-and-one

dash signals blinkered back. Captain Austin grinned
wryly, giving Helz the 'scope.

"We blew the invasion, kid. They'll be coming
out in that second banca we saw."

Gene Helz suffered a mixed emotion that dissolved
slowly to bewilderment. On the rock ledges above
the Victor sender was a sheet. Obviously, deduced
the skipper and exec of the submarine, there were
their guys. What in hell was holding up the show?
Two hours elapsed. The Victors stopped flashing.
Then the radio shack brought a message forward.

"Comsubs 7th Fleet, Captain. Our guys are in
position all right," the coding officer frowned, "but
they've got no boat!"

"No boat?" Austin exploded. "Then those were
Japs! They're laying for us and them. Gene," he
swiveled a look at the ensign commando, "you round
up your guys—on the double!"

Ten minutes later they were rigged and standing
by.

At dark *Redfin* made one long pass off Dent Haven
where Austin, routinely checking, opined that the
beach party would have little difficulty finding the
shore. Lights from Dent Haven supplied by the Japs
would beacon them in. The idea, Austin thought,
was to keep the hell away from the town and he
marked the range into the beach. There was nothing more to be said except the amenities, and Cy
Austin said them as his submarine broached and
the forward hatch was opened. On deck, as the raft
was swung over the side, he looked the four-man
party over.

"We'll back your play. Just holler. You're not
fighting any deadlines, men. You've got all night
and," he said softly, "should you have trouble and
not make it away with the Aussies, don't let it plague
your conscience. I want to go home with a full
complement. Good luck."

The sea was slack offshore, and the night was

darker than before. The four men climbed into their rubber raft and pushed away from the submarine. The current caught their boat as she edged toward the pale line of surf fifteen minutes later and for the first time one of them spoke:

"I must be chicken, Mister Helz," the radioman grunted. "I'm shakin' all over."

"That makes four of us in one boat," the ex-Marine shipped his paddle. "Sir, you see that beach-head now?"

"The peak?" Helz said. "No. We're under the beach now. She's blended with the horizon."

"Keep paddling!" the gunner growled. "Mister Helz, there's a hell of a current running off that surf. Feel it?"

"Yeah. Paddle, you guys!" the ensign snapped. "Kahler, stand by to send Victor—"

"I got the lamp in my lap," the radioman growled, digging with his makeshift paddle. "I make it about four hundred yards to the beach. Should I send now, sir?"

"Send."

The blinker tube clicked as the radioman held the light to his eye and focused on where he thought the range should be. The others paddled.

"Send it again. More to the left. We're in a rip here, drifting too fast," Ensign Helz whispered.

Kahler's finger triggered three dots, one dash. The beach was black beyond the fringing surf. Despite their paddling, the set continued working them right. Kahler looked sharply at Helz.

"Look! There it is!" Carrinder hissed. "There— way to the left!"

"Okay, dig for the beach," Helz ordered. "We'll burrow in there and they'll come down and meet us. Everybody—dig!"

Fifteen minutes later they were still paddling and the current was still setting them farther north. The coastline became indistinct so far as their contact was concerned, and after crossing the line of surf they lost it entirely. At the edge of the beach the four sailors sagged in their rubber raft, and on grounding, they hauled out the single length of tow rope and thought about the next phase.

"Kahler, you figure they're around that bend?"

"Yes, sir."

"Anybody think differently?"

Nobody did. Helz nodded to the radioman.

"I think we'll stick with this raft. Tow 'er. Let's try it."

With two of them on the beach, two in the water, they made slow progress along the deep edge of the Borneo coast. To the right was the black jungle, beyond rose the nebulous mountains now equally dark. Sticking to the raft was a unanimous idea. The raft was cumbersome, the mud thick and the tide an implacable enemy; even with four men towing, they could make slow headway at best. But it was their only tie with *Redfin*.

After twenty minutes the shore bent around in a wide arc. Off in the distance the *Redfin* party saw a sudden flickering of flame. Cautiously they waded on until finally, their legs and arms crippled by unaccustomed labors, the party stopped and, falling on the beach in exhaustion, speculated about the fire.

"That's our guys, Mister Helz," one of them said. "Maybe..."

"That's what I'm thinking," the ensign muttered grimly. "Suppose it isn't? Kahler! Get on that tube and blinker the boat, quick!"

The radioman pulled his blinker tube around then focused on the general area which they believed was their point of origin. A second after he sent his string of Vs, two lights, separated by thirty degrees, blinked back!

"Well, that does it, Mr. Helz," Carrinder growled. "One's *Redfin* and one's the Jap. What do we do?"

"I think," said the Californian, "we're flubbed

ducks. I don't know what the hell to do, but for sure we can't highball it out."

The unhappy prospects of boarding a Japanese patrol boat were resolved, momentarily, by Helz' decision to discontinue any further signaling. The next order of business, the ensign decided, was to contact the beach party of Anzacs, join forces and remain on the waterfront until the following night.

"I don't know what else we can do," the gunner's mate said miserably. "Those guys there are hung up too. Least we'll have company, sir."

"Yeah," Kahler rumbled. "But *whose?*"

It was easier to move the boat by paddling it, despite the heavy tide, so the four Navy men climbed in and dug their paddles. For an hour they inched along the current until, suddenly, a fire blazed directly opposite them, but quite far back from the beachhead. They paddled to the shore and Harrington and Kahler remained with the boat.

"I'll go ahead," Helz told the gunner. "You hang behind to the left and cover me."

The ruggedly built gunner's mate trudged up-beach, then flanked off and waited. Gene Helz moved alone toward the fire with his .45 out and the reassuring presence of the gunner's mate hunched over a BAR, Helz advanced slowly toward the cluster of figures silhouetted by the flames.

"Hello! You men at the fire!" the ensign yelled. "Come out. You're among friends—"

Something darted out of the jungle between Carrinder and the ensign. The figures at the fire dispersed. Abruptly a gun blasted out at the beachhead to Helz' right and Carrinder screamed:

"Japs! They're Japs!"

Hell broke loose at Dent Haven, North Borneo, and the first man to do anything about it was Carrinder. A Jap soldier bore down on him full tilt, rifle raised high to bayonet his throat. Carrinder squeezed

instinctively on the BAR trigger and the slugs threw
the charging Jap into reverse.

Helz tore across the beach to help Carrinder,
his .45 popping loudly over the clatter of the Browning. But Carrinder helped himself. He sidestepped
a second screaming Jap infantryman, twisted in the
sand and brought his BAR down across the Jap's
skull. As the soldier fell, Carrinder grabbed his rifle,
planted his foot in the middle of the squirming Jap's
back and drove the Jap's own bayonet between his
shoulder blades.

Helz moved in beside him, emptied the clip of his
.45, and two more Japanese fell at their feet, screaming and trying to push the blood back in the holes
in their stomachs. Others were charging down the
beach from the fire. Helz ejected the clip from his
.45 and shoved in another. Carrinder crouched and
turned the BAR on the newcomers. A line of his
slugs raced up the sand toward them. Another Jap
was slammed backward by the force of Carrinder's
.30s.

"I'm all right, Mister Helz," he yelled, while trying
to reload. "Let's get the hell out of here!"

Suddenly they heard firing from behind, between
them and the water. "God," Carrinder screamed and
spun on his heel, ready to empty the BAR.

It was Harrington and Kahler in the rubber boat,
backing them up with spotty Thompson fire, sending
slugs over their heads into the still-charging Japanese and at the others coming from the fire near the
jungle. Harrington and Kahler yelled, "Come on!
For Chrissakes, come on!" Helz shoved Carrinder,
and the two ducked low and stumbled toward the
rubber boat, tumbling into the bottom, panting. Then
the four of them waded the bobbing boat into the
surf, Carrinder firing the Browning wildly behind
him with one hand.

A wave shoved them back onto the beach.

"The tide's got us," Kahler screamed. "Goddammit, push!"

"Where the hell's the paddle, Harrington?" Helz grunted.

"It was here, sir."

"Sonofagun, there's only two now."

"Then paddle with your hands," Carrinder said.

The enemy appeared at the shoreline and, from the gun emplacements at Dent Haven, Jap heavy-caliber fire and star shells began exploding over the shore. The fireworks showed them an enemy rubber boat approximately the size of their own. The four men scrambled in their own bobbing craft, Kahler lunging forward with his blinker tube, Helz in the stern and the other two balancing amidships. The tide was no longer slack. At a full, brisk four to six knots, it swept over the coral reef and piled combers chaotically into the boat. Kahler took a sea over his head, cursed as the flashlight in his jacket suddenly snapped on.

Whining steel punched geysers of water in the surf as Kahler, howling, clawed at his jacket and tore the light off. It sank slowly, giving the enemy boat enough time to pinpoint them. They rowed silently with their hands, gun butts and blinker tube. Then Kahler sent a string of Vs. *Two* lights flashed back. Behind them the dark shadow of a rubber boat drew closer.

In the sea passage, a motor rumbled malevolently behind them and a light flashed brightly. Jap gunners fell short with their three-inch stuff. The four raiders, praying and digging, made their boat fairly skim through the troughs.

"Is it ours or theirs?" Harrington groaned.

"I can't tell!" Kahler snarled. "Hand me a gun."

"*Redfin, Redfin!*" Carrinder screamed. "Is that you?"

"Bring her in, Helz! We'll cover you."

"Start covering! They're right behind us!"

The rubber boat bumped against the high steel
sides of the submarine. Enemy gunfire lifted, veil-
ing the breaking surf in an eerie yellow light. The
four men in the rubber boat cut loose simultaneously
at the enemy craft in their wake. The Japs cursed
and fired back, the rattle of bullets pounding *Redfin's* diving planes.

They were still firing and being hauled aboard,
slipping, scrambling frantically as the enemy boat
smashed against the submarine bow. Japs scrambled
along the sides, holding to the flukes and triggering
their weapons while half overboard. The four sailors,
backed by men on deck who didn't dare fire for fear
of hitting them, finished off the Japanese invaders.
When the last enemy soldier was pushed overboard,
Redfin's crew hustled the frustrated, beat-up raiders
down the tower to sanctuary. The submarine dived.
The six Aussie coast-watchers stayed put until *Harder* took them off two months later.

In the entire war of the submarines, only once
did the enemy attempt to board. And only once were
they repelled. That unique pleasure belonged to a
quartet of pig-boaters led by a kid ensign. In time
the Navy recognized their effort, the three enlisted
men receiving awards and Gene Helz receiving the
Navy Cross for extraordinary heroism under the
damnedest fire that ever came out of a nothing place
called Dent Haven, North Borneo.

TANG

"CAPTAIN to the bridge! Radar contact!"

The strident rasping of the squawk box in the cramped wardroom of the submarine *Tang* instantly brought Commander Richard O'Kane, USN, to his feet. The tall, rugged young skipper of one of the hottest fleet-subs in the South Pacific was nursing a cup of black coffee and brooding on a conspicuous lack of enemy merchant shipping in Formosa Straits.

Slamming out of the wardroom a step ahead of Lieutenant Murray Frazee, the exec, O'Kane, raced aft to the conning tower ladder. A moment later, O'Kane was poised at the back of a tense radar operator. Seaman 1/c George Hallahan was pointing to the recorder: yellow blobs of flickering light slowly moved across the dark screen.

"Convoy, Captain," Hallahan muttered. "Range 7500 yards, speed 9 knots. I can tell you how many ships when the range comes down—"

The course was converging. *Tang's* skipper knew he could wait out the arrival of the convoy by merely submerging to periscope depth. Instead, with characteristic aggressiveness, O'Kane swiveled around to Frazee and grunted:

"Tell the OOD to ring up flank speed! Let's go take a look at that damned convoy!"

The exec responded by thundering halfway up the bridge ladder so that only the top of his head appeared in the darkness. There was a sharp bawling of orders and bells were sounded in the control room. An electric charge surged through the compartments of the sub as *Tang* leaped ahead. Ten seconds later, the general alarm sent crewmen racing to battle stations.

A messenger hurried to the conning tower with the skipper's light jacket and binoculars. Then O'Kane went up to the bridge and stood behind a spray shield looking at the night. In the forward room, an alert soundman reported the steady thum of heavy screws dead ahead. In the periscope's heart four lookouts watched the horizon, ready.

"Surface torpedo attack! Make ready the bow tubes!" O'Kane tersely intoned to the talker beside him on the bridge.

In two minutes, the converging range was down to 5500 yards and sound began to pick up the faster, tinnier screws of the escorts. Hallahan began feeding ranges and speed with regularity to Frazee, rapidly twisting in a correct torpedo solution into the torpedo data computer. The sub bounded ahead like an eager shark boring in for the kill.

Bare-headed, peering anxiously into the night, Commander O'Kane stood beside the OOD, Lieutenant [jg] J. M. Tompson, with his glasses fixed to his slate-gray eyes. Above the submarine officers were the lookouts. Abruptly one of the enlisted men leaned down:

"Targets bearing two points on the starboard bow, Captain!"

O'Kane swiveled his gaze. Then he saw them. At that moment, the radar man called up: there were at least seven ships, he said, including the escorts.

"Standby forward!" O'Kane snapped. "Standby aft!"

The telephone man was now on the conning tower

ladder, repeating Commander O'Kane's orders vocally with subdued shouts to the control room. All was in readiness as Frazee relayed the word that he had a good solution in the TDC. The range closed inexorably until it was down to 1200 yards. Still, O'Kane was silent. Finally, when the *Tang's* skipper could make out the bare outlines of a tanker and transport inside the screen, he wheeled around to the white-faced talker.

"Ask the exec when I can fire!" said O'Kane.

"You may fire any time," came the reply:

"Very well," O'Kane said. He took a visual sighting on the first ship, sucked in his breath and nodded. *"Fire one! Fire two! Fire three!"*

The submarine lurched drunkenly as she skidded to Slow and three "pickles" surged from the forward torpedo room to the nearest Jap ship. A jagged sear of light roared across the sky forty seconds later as the first torpedo hit. The second missed, but the third bored in the vitals of the transports. Now O'Kane saw other targets by the bizarre flashes of light.

"Fire four! Fire five!" he hissed. *"Come left ... there! Fire six!"*

Three more bundles of death speared out into the black waters and rushed to Japanese shipping bound for Leyte Gulf. O'Kane ordered the submarine turned around to aim the torpedoes in his stern tubes.

All hell was breaking loose in the convoy.

Milling around in frenzied confusion to avoid torpedoes, the Japs had lost all semblance of order and were rushing to break formation. The night sky was sundered by terrible, jagged explosions and flames from an oil tanker shot up hundreds of feet into the air to illumine the ghostly scene. By the light of the flames, Japanes lookouts spotted the submarine in their midst. Abruptly tongues of red and white death spilled from gun barrels and the wild path of tracers roared over the *Tang*.

"Fire seven! Fire eight! Fire nine! Fire ten!" O'Kane ordered quickly, pacing the flow of torpedoes with an omnipresent stopwatch. "Now let's get the hell out of here! All ahead full . . ."

Tang responded accordingly. Bearing under the hull of one sinking transport and slicing around the side of another, O'Kane took the submarine away from the gun-happy escorts. Bearing out at right full rudder on four main engines, the grinning skipper of the sub ordered the lookouts down from the shears for their own safety. Only he and the OOD stood on the bridge watching the particolored pyrotechnics of the exploding Japanese ships.

"I figured we pickled four or five!" O'Kane snapped. "Let's go out for a reload and get some of those Goddamned escorts . . ."

So he did.

It was 2100 October 24, 1944, a hot muggy night. *Tang's* memorable fifth war patrol under Commander Dick O'Kane was to be a symphony of death which neither the Japs nor the American submarine force would ever forget.

Richard Heatherington O'Kane, Annapolis '34, came by his skills honestly. As the former exec of the *Wahoo*, under the command of daring, jut-jawed Commander Dudley "Mush" Morton, O'Kane in his role of second-in-command had carved a unique and enviable niche for himself during *Wahoo's* fantastic battles with Japanese convoys. Morton, who was famous for reckless and impossible torpedo attacks on enemy destroyers, claimed that O'Kane was "the bravest man I've ever met. Who else would look at a Jap destroyer rushing down our throats as we submerged?"

The spirit of the *Wahoo* went deep in the fighting disposition of the young exec. But one day O'Kane received a transfer and a promotion. The great team of Morton and O'Kane was irretrievably broken up by the growing submarine war. O'Kane was urgently needed to take out the *Tang,* and his old pig-boat the *Wahoo,* went to sea without him.

It never returned.

Early in February, 1944, a battle-tested and vengeful O'Kane sailed his submarine from Midway Island with a full load of torpedoes and equally full load of hatred for anything Japanese. On the seventeenth, off the naval base of Palau, O'Kane's lookouts spotted the distant smoke of a convoy. After several hours of jockeying into position, eight ships were spotted. O'Kane dove and prepared to send a spread of torpedoes veering toward a fat-bellied tanker in the van. His war was beginning.

Using a conventional day torpedo attack, the skipper brought his tub to sixty-three feet, periscope depth, timing an order to shoot at ten second intervals. The convoy was bathed in twilight sun, sailing along placidly and ever so often zigzagging lackadaisically. Of the eight ships, only two were escorts—small destroyer escorts that submariners deprecated as "spitkits." O'Kane was hunched over the lenset as the voice of Frazee called up to the conning tower:

"You've got a perfect setup, Captain. You can pluck 'em off like ripe grapes . . ."

O'Kane was no stickler for protocol. Nor did he demand it of any of his men. He brushed his black, sweaty hair from his eyes and growled:

"Tell Frazee he can give me bearings to those escorts first. If we get rid of those sonuvbitches, we can pick off the rest at leisure."

The "word" was repeated verbatim.

Now O'Kane plastered his face to the periscope, and snapped out the orders that dispatched four perfectly timed torpedoes from the forward room. The first three hit, bathing the twilight sky in a cherry-red glow as the tanker crumpled and disappeared.

The skipper was still watching as the soundman's voice boomed out of the squawk box:

"Screws—fast screws, Captain! Bearing zero zero ten!"

"Take her down deep! Right full rudder!" O'Kane snapped.

Tang responded as a destroyer escort, bearing down with a bone in her teeth, charged over the spot where *Goyoten Maru* had disappeared in a welter of bubbles and foam. Next came the depth charges and *Tang*, no longer a virgin, took her first pasting since departing the ways and dipping her plunging bows to the sea. She had come of age.

The first patrol ended four ships and thirty-three days later, when O'Kane brought his submarine back to Pearl Harbor. There, he received the congratulations of Rear Admiral Lockwood and another assignment. Mush Morton's old exec received the first of *five* Navy Crosses from Lockwood and, after a brief rest, took off again for Midway.

O'Kane wanted action and the Palau sea lanes seemed the logical place. The second war patrol, however, proved a great disappointment as shipping had abruptly stopped in that area. For better than sixty days, O'Kane's outer torpedo doors remained shut and sailors groused for want of ships to kill. O'Kane groused along with them, cursing the area that he himself had voluntarily chosen. The only thing of significance that happened, so far as O'Kane was concerned, was making a rendezvous with the badly damaged *Trigger*.

This submarine had taken a brutal pounding from Jap escorts while attacking a convoy. As a consequence, she had popped a number of vital gaskets and was leaking badly. Altogether *Trigger* was a mess, with her fuel lines ruptured, her pump room flooded and her outer doors jammed up forward. Hasty repairs were made when *Tang* gave over virtually all her spare parts.

It was during this time that O'Kane received a radio message to take the *Tang* to Truk, to standby the big Jap naval base for lifeguard work during an American air strike. O'Kane didn't particularly like the direction, but it was better than sticking around and watching an empty ocean.

O'Kane was never particularly happy unless he was firing torpedoes, but the saving of twenty-three airmen who'd ditched in the Pacific was a hazardous (at times) chore that broke the monotony of the long cruise. He left Truk for Midway with "overcrowded bunks and damned low on fuel. Also no ships sunk."

"Targets! Bearing zero six five—15,000 yards!" The cry to action stations that came abruptly on *Tang's* third war patrol began an attack during which O'Kane commendably managed to put down ten ships. He wiped out, in fact, the entire convoy including escorts. It was *Tang's* first unabashed show of fury (of any real magnitude) and a definite indication of things to come. For this patrol, O'Kane and crew received the first of two Presidential Unit Citations.

Taking on a fresh load of torpedoes, O'Kane stormed out into the war zone and knocked off two more Japanese ships before another grisly lull set in. So went patrol number four. It was highly significant only insofar as the terrible punishment suffered from relentless screen ships made all hands realize there were *two* sides playing the game, and the other side could dish out crippling depth charges galore. After a couple of eight-hour shellackings from Fubuki-class destroyers, *Tang* limped home licking her wounds.

But Richard Heatherington O'Kane's attitude now remained virtually unchanged. He commented to his exec during the refit: "If we sink even *one* ship, this bucket can take anything they throw at us and it's worth it. The hell with the ash cans. I want targets..."

He found a number of them in the East China Sea area on the ill-fated two part fifth patrol.

Ordered out in early October, 1944, O'Kane drew Formosa Strait and promptly fired at two destroyers and an enemy light cruiser. Next he went rampaging along the shore and exchanged shots with enemy installations guarding the inland sea. But finally, there came the day when there were masts on the horizon and O'Kane passed the word for night torpedo attack.

There were merchantmen and escorts. *Tang*, doing an end-around, waited for the convoy to pass. Then he penetrated the screen and disregarding everything he had told his men about caution, went in and fired torpedoes at escorts and merchantmen alike. In fact, during this first phase of the patrol, O'Kane even exchanged shots with a "spitkit that intended working us over." Seven ships were credited to the *Tang* for a long, but thoroughly enjoyable night's work.

Then the targets stopped coming and Richard Heatherington O'Kane grew restless. Deeper penetration into Formosa Strait, he reasoned, would probably bring down more depth charges. Half the Japanese war fleet was looking for *Tang* and O'Kane knew it. But he was faced with the prospect of going home with unfired torpedoes and he didn't especially like it.

"We go in until we find ships, Goddammit!" he sullenly told his exec twenty days after he'd sunk the last Jap ship. "I can't take this doing nothing any more—"

Frazee complied by bending on all four mains until *Tang* was deep in enemy territory. Nothing happened for a few nights. Planes were spotted and each time *Tang* dove, but her implacid skipper refused to quit the area.

Precisely at 2100 October 24, 1944, *Tang's* luck changed ... for the worse. A convoy hopped onto the radar screen into the night sea and O'Kane, eager to sink ships, charged straight toward the convoy.

Ten torpedoes were fired in rapid succession from the bow and stern tubes. Then, O'Kane, amid the voluminous explosions of Japanese fires, bore away for reload.

O'Kane ordered the remaining two torpedoes made ready.

"We're going back and finish off that transport!" he yelled down to the conning tower. "Never mind the ranges. I can see where they are by their fires—"

Now the night was filled with wild orange light and the little submarine, twenty minutes later, turned around and faced her attackers. Boring in at full speed, O'Kane made straight for the cripple and ordered the engines stopped. Five seconds later, the outer torpedo doors jolted open and the murder-mad skipper glowered down for a visual sighting.

"You ought to see this bonfire!" O'Kane shouted from his sighting position. Sweat poured from his excited body as he ordered the *Tang* to come around on a perpendicular course. The tall, rough-talking CO stood on the bridge with just a handful of his awestruck officers and men. There was no particular reason for the submarine to hide at periscope depth, no earthly reason for a torpedo to run erratically.

And yet that's exactly what happened to the ace sub in the war zone.

Grabbing his stop watch, Richard Heatherington O'Kane snapped out the battle order that was to doom his craft and all but the bridge personnel to either a watery grave or prison camp.

"Standby!" O'Kane hissed.

The night was filled with milling, sinking ships and destroyer escorts bobbing and weaving between. Flame from an oil tanker that hadn't gone down roared into the moonless sky hundreds of feet in the air. Grimly, O'Kane watched the havoc he'd caused.

A sheen of perspiration stood out on his forehead and he brushed it away with the flat of his hand.

"Standby for shoot."

"Standing by!" came the word from the telephone man.

"Fire one! Fire two!"

Twin spirals of instant death lunged from the bow of the submarine. At this moment, Japanese machine gunners on the destroyer escorts again picked up the dark silhouette of the raider and red and yellow tongues of flame spewed out into the darkness. O'Kane ignored the shooting. He stood on the bridge watching the timed path of the last two torpedoes.

From the conning tower came the bone-chilling word:

"Circular run! Circular, Captain!"

The horror in the man's voice duplicated the horror in O'Kane's eyes as he watched one of the phosphorescent streaks suddenly porpoise and veer sharply around.

The fish was circling left as O'Kane barked, "Right full rudder—ahead emergency!"

But the submarine complied too late. The second and last torpedo slammed into the stern and she was enveloped in a tremendous flame.

On the bridge, all hands were knocked overboard by the jarring concussion of the blow. Concussion immediately killed all power and sent the mortally wounded fleet-type submarine to the bottom. *Tang* setled at 180 feet with fire raging in all compartments.

For Richard Heatherington O'Kane, it was nearly —but not quite—over. He found himself swimming furiously in a burning sea—swimming toward a group of men. The first torpedo had broken the back of an enemy transport. Men were leaping into the water and destroyer escorts were milling around trying to recover survivors.

O'Kane joined a group of four swimmers [the

others had separated from the group] and the four men heard their CO yell:

"She's gone! She's gone—swim for the Jap!"

The quartet of swimmers struck out for an enemy DE, rounding one of the sinking ships. By the bizarre light of the flames, the men were seen and the destroyer hove to. Lines were dropped and the choking, half-drowned remnants of the *Tang* pulled desperately for the enemy warship.

"I seen some more guys!" someone yelled.

O'Kane yelled back: "Keep together—swim. You can't help anybody but yourself—"

The Jap hovered above them finally and the four men caught the lines and were taken aboard, gasping and oil-soaked. O'Kane's trip was over. He was stripped and with three other prisoners ordered to attention. Then, by the firelight, Japanese "interrogation" began. First came fists, then bayonets brought down across the backs of the agonized Americans. O'Kane took his punishment, in silence, and refused to divulge any vital information, not that the Japanese expected any.

Meanwhile, the *Tang* lay on the bottom with her after torpedo room stove in and electrical fires gutting her forward room. The men who hadn't died outright in the sinking fought their way forward to first battle the fires in the torpedo room and then to pry open the sub's escape hatch. Of the thirteen escapees to reach the surface, only five managed to stay alive until morning when they were picked up by a Japanese patrol boat.

O'Kane and his men fared a little better. Treated to savage beatings and water cures by the Imperial Navy, O'Kane was taken to an enemy prison camp on the mainland to sit out the balance of the war. He later told correspondents that the beatings weren't too hard to take inasmuch as they were being administered by the men he had just torpedoed and those he might have, had the fish · rushed in straight, hot and true.

There the story of the *Tang* ended. Upon repatriation, Commander Richard Heatherington O'Kane was flown to the States where he received the Congressional Medal of Honor from President Truman. He also received another stripe, and upon his resignation from the Navy held the rank of Rear Admiral.

No submarine skipper in the war against Japan could have done more.

FIRST BLOOD AT LEYTE GULF

"Standby forward! Make ready the bow tubes—" Commander Dave McClintock growled tersely, pulling his eyes from the periscope. "Take her down to sixty-three feet. Let's go—fast!"

USS *Darter* dipped gracefully beneath the deep blue water of Palawan Passage, south of the Philippines. The feather of white wake caused by her receding periscope evoked no violent reaction from the Japanese task force rapidly closing on a shooting course.

"Fast screws, sir! Bearing one seven zero, sir!"

"Mark the bearing! Snap it up, forward! Goddammit, snap it up!" Dave McClintock snarled, upflexing the handles of the periscope and crouching again.

"Forward room reports readiness, sir!" the conning tower J-1 talker rasped softly.

McClintock rammed a sweaty fist into both eyes, tightened his jaw and roared, "Come to sixty-three feet! We connect now, gents, and we're squared away properly for December seventh. Holy Cow! What a setup—"

Battleships, heavy and light cruisers, and destroyers suddenly materialized in *Darter's* scope, filling it. Commander McClintock's voice went to a hoarse whisper as he snapped out his battle orders. The outer torpedo doors forward banged open in muffled compliance.

"Up 'scope! Bearing . . . mark! Standby to fire—*fire!*"

The submarine lurched, settled. McClintock blinked at the fattest target, last warship in the second column closing him rapidly. "Mark the bearing! *Fire Two. Fire Three! Fire Four! Fire Five!* Take her down—*dive Dive!*"

McClintock was silent, perspiration pouring from his arms as he stared at the stop watch, timing the torpedo runs. At 2,800 yards with targets closing at fifteen knots, it would be only a few moments before the explosions would start coming. McClintock sucked in his breath, and *Darter* went deep . . .

It was just 0700 October 23, 1944, seven hours after Dave McClintock first made contact with three enemy ships. The previous morning before submerging, *Darter's* radio picked up a news broadcast of MacArthur's landing on Leyte. "Way I see it," McClintock smiled speculatively, "the Jap fleet should be hightailing it out of Singapore about now—probably looking for a shortcut to Leyte-Balabac Strait. Let's get the hell out of this area and go hunting!"

And so he did. And his premise was right to begin with—except that there was a good deal more to the events immediately to follow than Dave McClintock could possibly deduce.

Five days before, on October 18, First Admiral Toyada—Yamamoto's successor—decisively committed his main line warships to a fight to the death. It was the last ditch stand of the Empire. With MacArthur's landing in the Philippines imminent, Toyada, without hesitation, decided to take on the American fleet while simultaneously protecting southeast oil interests. The name of the plan was Operation *Sho*-One—"Conquer!"

Going strictly by the book Operation *Sho*-One

couldn't fail. Unfortunately for Toyada, nobody on Halsey's staff was quite willing to believe it. At 2300, October 22, Vice Admiral Takeo Kurita, commanding the Imperial Navy Force that consisted of the titantic *Yamato,* world's largest battleship, and the *Mushashi,* also another secretly armed eighteen-inch dreadnaught, three smaller battleships, twelve heavy and light cruisers and a screening force of fourteen destroyers, put out from the Singalese base of Lingga bound on a speed run for the Philippines.

Admiral Kurita, a veteran of thirty-eight years in the naval service, knew his stuff. The success or failure of the plan very largely depended on him and whether the First Diversion Attack Force got through or not. *Sho*-One was certainly a desperate plan, and a dangerous one, but it was the only one the Japanese could have adopted at the time. When Kurita's Attack Force departed Brunei Bay on the morning of October 22, the timetable was set. The admiral would advance along the west side of the narrow Palawan Passage at a speed of sixteen knots; thereafter he would turn eastward and circle to the south of Mindoro on the twenty-third, increasing speed at this time to twenty-four knots; lastly, at sundown of the same day he would arrive at the eastern entrance of San Bernadino Straits, turn south, sweep down the coast of Somar, and have gone on A-day, October 24, into Leyte Gulf.

It was a formidable armada, the greatest mass of concentrated firepower yet seen in the Pacific War. Such was Operation *Sho*-One, the Empire's last ditch stand to hold the gains of a long and costly war. And, at the same time, to whip the elusive American fleet once and for all. The plan was foolproof, except for minor—so-called—details.

Operation Conquer was a two-part Sunday punch, a wallop that depended on the complete coordination of two separate forces once the fleet reached the northeast coast of Borneo. Splitting his gargantuan

assembly at that juncture, Kurita committed two
overage battleships, the revamped heavy cruiser
Mogami and four destroyers to the custody of Vice
Admiral Nishimura's "C" Force. The second force,
the First Diversion Attack Force, commanded by
Kurita himself, and Nishimura's line of warships,
were to sail in a planned pincers movement on the
American transports in Leyte Gulf.

The wheels were turning, really turning. Kurita
topped off with fuel at Brunei Bay on the north
coast. If he could bag the transports, the proposed
Philippine invasion would come to naught and, more
than likely, so would a goodly chunk of American
shipping.

But there was one remotely possible hitch to the
Imperial Fleet Admiral's grand *coup de main*—the
American Third Fleet under Halsey. And while, ad-
mittedly, the U.S. battlewagons couldn't hope to swap
Sunday punches with Japanese first-liners, the
American Task Force had a few other things going
for it. Namely: Five [one hundred plane capacity]
carriers, six jeep [thirty-three-plane capacity] carriers, six new battleships, seven light cruisers, two
heavies and forty-six destroyers. Indeed, this was an
armada to reckon with—but the wily Kurita had no
particular intention of doing so.

To lure the United States Navy out of his path,
Kurita provided for a seemingly luscious bait of
several retread carriers under Niguchi Ozawa, *Sho*-
plan's sacrificial lamb.

So it was, then, that Kurita's main body quietly
slipped out of the Borneo sanctuary after topping
off with fuel. Under cover of a black night, the twen-
ty-second of October, one hour before midnight,
he hitched his battle flag to the yard of the heavy
cruiser *Agato* and steamed in two columns for a
rendezvous with fate.

The morning of the twenty-third was gray, the
slick calm of the Pacific so silent that Admiral Ku-

rita could balance a cup of bilious tea on one finger
and still not spill a drop. He was satisfied for the moment. All had gone well during the night and Admiral Koyangi stood beside him telling him as much.
Kurita's movements were shielded. Effectively he
could sidestep the American fleet, blast the transports in Leyte Gulf to flaming eternity and, more
than likely, discourage future attempts to take Leyte
Gulf. Each flotilla was composed of a double column
of heavy ships with the cruisers naturally in the
van. Around the entire squadron were whole formations of destroyers, buzzing violently. Admiral
Kurita's tea was finished ...

Aboard the submarine *Darter*, Dave McClintock
commanded. The speed run to Balabac Strait had
justified his judgment. Three enemy surface contacts
smeared brightly in his radar screen, but despite
everything his engineers could get out of four mains,
the Japanese warships pulled away from him. Aban-
doning pursuit, McClintock moved south for a quick
rendezvous with Commander Bladen Claggett of the
Dace.

At 0017 both subs were running a parallel course,
the commanding officers conversing by megaphone.
Dave McClintock felt miserable. Three juicy "pips"
on his SC scope—lost! It was a rotten way to climax
a war patrol, McClintock growled disgustedly. Claggett of *Dace* sympathized.

Suddenly McClintock's head swiveled around. The
bridge speaker erupted: "Radar contact! One three
one, true, thirty thousand yards—contact is doubtful
—probably rain cloud, sir!"

"Rain cloud like hell! That's the Jap Fleet!" Mc-
Clintock snarled. He shoved his face back in the
megaphone and gave Claggett the range and bearing
of ships "too numerous to mention."

Both submarines charged forward, all mains bent
on. Soon enemy ships appeared stretched out in Palawan Passage, headed north. *Darter* broke radio si-

lence to make three contact reports to CSP at Pearl Harbor. He reported eleven ships. There were thirty-one, actually. It was McClintock's plan to get ahead of the convoy and take station on the port side; Claggett would take the starboard flank. Enemy speed was constant at fifteen knots and the submarines, pushing twenty, slowly rushed ahead for a dawn periscope attack.

At 0425 *Darter* was ten miles ahead on the port flank. Five minutes later, all hands were called to coffee. At 0500 minus ten, battle stations! sounded in the waiting submarine. Dave McClintock stalked his control room like a sullen tiger, checking his watch ... twenty minutes— twenty eternities more—fifteen eternities ... A tense hush fell on *Darter's* control room as she went to a westerly course for a down the throat shot at the task force. The rest of the time was spent at deep submergence, three hundred feet below.

Dave McClintock finally checked the clock and rasped out his orders. *Darter* came to periscope depth and a thick pencil streak of a wake pierced the surface slick. The staggering sight that every submariner dreams about faced the commander. He swung the scope quickly, his breath sharp, his eyes riveted to the larger forms occupying the rear of the two columns. One may suppose that McClintock, seeing all this steel booty, proclaimed in no uncertain terms:

"God Almighty! Good Holy Smokes! It can't be— it's the whole blasted Jap Navy!"

The periscope came down. It went up again at 0527. At 0527, the first four ships in the east column were positively identified as cruisers, the last, a late-model battlewagon.

It is most absorbing to quote directly from the Commander's fascinating battle report which tells the story of this interesting phase of the battle that is to follow:

0528: Range is 2,800 yards to the first cruiser in column.

0532: Commence firing bow tubes at leading cruiser. After firing two into him and one straight ahead, target was rearing by so close that we couldn't miss, so spread the remainder inside his length. Then swung hard left [to bring stern tubes to bear for him while getting set up on the second cruiser].

0533: Torpedo started hitting the first cruiser five hits. Commenced firing stern tubes at second cruiser. With periscope back to first target to see the sight of a lifetime. [Cruiser was so close that all of her could not be seen at once with periscope in high power]. She was a mass of billowing black smoke from the Number One turret to the stern. No superstructure could be seen. Bright orange flames shot out from the side along the main deck from the bow, which was dipping under. Number One turret was at water level. She was definitely finished. Five hits had her sinking and in flames. It was estimated that there were few, if any, survivors.

0534: Started deep. Evaded. Heard four hits in second cruiser. Felt certain that four hits would sink this one too.

0539: Depth charge attacked again. Four destroyers milling about overhead. Commenced hearing breaking up noises on sound gear, roughly where the targets should have stopped. Noise could be heard throughout hull and all compartments. They increased until they seemed to be right overhead and shook the submarine violently. Heavy rumblings and explosions.

0557: Heard four distinct torpedo explosions in rapid succession. Probably *Dace* firing. Japs must think our submarines are everywhere at once.

From 0600 to 0604 there were tremendous explo-

sions, probably magazines. It is estimated that
from 0600 our target's breaking up noises began to combine with those of *Dace's* targets.
0605: Depth charges began again. Probably meant
for *Dace* this time. A total of about thirty-six
were heard. Heard the sound of more breaking up noises and distant rumbling explosions
[not depth charges] until about 0625.
0630: Last of the depth charges."

The intrepid submarine moved in for the kill.

"Shooting bearing! Mark the bearing—*Fire One!
Fire Two! Fire Three! Fire Four! Fire Five! Fire
Six!*"

Dave McClintock snarled venomously, "Flagship's
signaling with her searchlight, dammit. Probably
seen our torpedo wakes..."

The light shuttered out abruptly a moment later.

Freezing sweat plastered McClintock's shirt to his
chest, his eyes ran with salty perspiration from his
hairline.

"Shift targets to second cruiser. Mark the bearing!"

"Range, fifteen thousand yards to second cruiser,
sir!" Lieutenant Gene Wilkinson, the TCS operator
bawled. "TCS is ready. Bearing, Mark! *Fire Seven*—"

Darter lurched off target drunkenly as the first
underwater concussion rocked her. The force of the
explosion tore the scope away from McClintock's
hands, sending a vibratory shock down his arms.
Somebody yelled, "Depth charges!"

Dave McClintock yelled back, "Depth charges, my
a—"

The first explosion was a torpedo bashing in Admiral Kurita's flagship, forward. Kurita spilled his
tea. There were five hits as the cruiser *Agato,* suddenly stopped dead in the sea, billowing a giant mush-
room of black smoke and flame. Suddenly she was
down by the bow, but Dave McClintock, his knees

trembling, his lean wet body clinging to the periscope handles, moved to finish his second target.

"Fire Eight! Fire Nine! Fire Ten!" McClintock screamed. "Take her down—rig for silent running! Take her down, goddammit..."

Darter went deep, all machinery stopped for silent running, the men of Dave McClintock's pigboat silently waiting for the punishment which was sure to come. Five minutes later, the Jap destroyers swarmed angrily down the submariner's line of escape, depth charging avidly. Dave McClintock held the overhead, his body glued to the scope tube. Time evanesced slowly as the heat rose precipitously in the boat. Darter stayed intact despite a thorough going by Kurita's DDs.

At 0820 Darter's log recorded the following:

"At periscope depth: Ashio-class cruiser sighted, range 12,000 yards, at our attack position, listing slightly to starboard and dead in the water. No steam up. Three destroyers were near him and three planes circled the vicinity. No smoke coming from the cruiser."

On Claggett's Dace were similar moments of near fantasy for a submariner. Peering into his sweat-soaked periscope, Commander Claggett blinked numbly at a congregation of battleships, heavy and light cruisers and destroyers—a task force! Something not a dozen submarines would ever be privileged to see. Dace lined up.

At 0552 Dace's log recorded the following:

"The two cruisers passed ahead at about 1500 yards. They were overlapping, appearing to be running screen for my target—an Ise-class battleship! Had a beautiful view of them and identified them positively as the Jap Nachi-class ships. My target can be seen better now, and appears to be a Kongo-class battleship. He looks larger than the two cruisers that have just passed ahead. He had two stacks and superstructure appears much heavier. Sound also reports target screws as heavier and slower than those of cruisers."

At 0054 *Dace's* log recorded the following:

"Commenced firing a salvo of six bow tubes. Fired One, Two, Three, Four, Five, Six. Took quick look around and saw next battleship still close, so started deep, turning into this wake. And another salvo one minute later: First hit! Second hit! Third hit! Fourth hit!"

Dace's target became a sheet of flame from stem to stern, with a succession of violent internal explosions literally tearing her apart. To her soundman, it sounded "as if the bottom of the ocean were blowing up!" Nothing, Captain Claggett of *Dace* observed tensely, could cause this much noise except magazines exploding. Nothing, did, either.

Eight hours later, the two American submarines chased down a radar contact. One Jap cripple, a cruiser of the *Atago* class guarded by two tin cans, was limping for port. *Darter* closed first. The chase continued through the balance of the day, trying to penetrate the cruiser's screen. Finally, at 0085, Dave McClintock's intrepid pigboat recorded its last entry. The following is the verbatim account of Commander McClintock:

"That night, October 24, 1944, *Darter* and *Dace* were again standing side by side to finish off the cruiser. We thought she would be towed inside the Palawan Bay. Instead, she got under way, making about five to eight knots southwest. The *Dace* started 'ending the round' to the east and *Darter* to the west.

"At midnight we had about an hour to go to gain position for attack ahead of the cruiser. The OOD, Lieutenant Ed Skorupski, and I were on the bridge in the pitch black night. At about five minutes past ten we were making seventeen knots, trying to attack before the cruiser could pick up more speed. The navigator was in the conning tower; all officers and most of the crew were at battle stations.

"Something happened! We hit something and we were riding over it as a whale noses up out of the water. We took a large up-angle and the stern went under as far as the engine hatch. Then all of a sudden the stern rode up and we came to rest high and dry.

" 'What was that?' the navigator yelled, running to the bridge. I told him we were aground. He jumped into the conning tower to check the chart, and was back on the bridge in a minute. 'Captain, it can't be that we are aground—the nearest land is nineteen miles away.' But we were aground just the same on an uncharted reef.

"A Japanese destroyer with the cruisers started closing in coming closer and closer until the range was 4,000 yards. That may not sound so close on shore, but it sounded close then to us, sitting on that reef with nothing but one four-ranger and a couple of pop guns. When the Jap destroyer faded on our radar, we breathed a little easier, and went to work in the hope of pulling off at high tide. It was then or never as far as getting off that reef was concerned.

"It was get off by dawn or fight the Jap destroyers and airplanes. Using bunker lights, we had signaled the *Dace* shortly after running aground, and she abandoned her chase of the cruiser to try to pull us off.

"We gave up about two-thirty; we were high and dry. Down below all equipment was destroyed. Sledgehammers were used on the radar and radios. Confidential gear was burned, choking everybody with smoke.

"At 0300 we commenced to abandon ship.

"Captain Claggett brought the *Dace* right up to the edge of the shoal. After setting the demolition charge, time clock in the control room, I went topside and was last to leave the *Darter*."

Dace removed the ill-fated submarine's personnel, and fired a spread of torpedoes at her which exploded prematurely on the reef. Still defying torpedoes six days later, the huge submarine *Nautilus* was shipped to the scene and eventually demolished *Darter* after pumping fifty-six 6-inch shells into her hulk.

Thus ended one of the wildest hunts of the submarine war, an epochal event that the enemy never forgot with good reason.

THE LAST PATROL OF THE HALIBUT

Luzon Strait was calm, brassy with October sunlight. On the bridge of the submarine *Halibut,* Commander Ignatius J. "Pete" Galantin was squinting through binoculars for signs of an air battle somewhere off Cape Engano, P.T., between Halsey's carrier planes and a Jap fleet. The sub, making her tenth war patrol as a member of Roach's Raiders —a three-boat wolfpack—was hunting for strays.

Standing beside the skipper were Lieutenant Commander Guy Gugliotta, the exec, and Ensign W. N. Kendall, the OOD. Lookouts were posted above in the periscope shears. Time: five twenty-five. An hour earlier, the sound of bombing had been heard through the hull and, acting on this cue, Galantin had ordered flank speed and the setting of a VHF watch below in the radio shack. These steps abruptly began to pay off.

"Captain," a messenger appeared on the conning tower ladder, "Lieutenant Conant says to tell you that planes are coming through loud and clear. They're working over Japs somewhere around here—"

Galantin, thirty-four—rangy, good looking—acknowledged curtly and swiveled around to the shears.

"Lookouts!" he bawled. "Targets out there!"

122   DIVE, DIVE!

Below, Jim Conant was turning up the gain on the VHF for the express benefit of startled bluejackets wedged in the doorway of the miniscule radio shack. Howling in over the airwaves was a blow-by-blow of Third Fleet flyboys attacking an *"Ise-*class battleship and two cruisers." Above the cacophony of diving planes and heavy caliber fire, pilots were ranting ecstatically. Loud and clear were the reports: "There they are below us—dive! Dive!—Yippee! I got me a battlewagon!"

On the bridge, simultaneously, a lookout spotted a puff of brown smoke on the horizon, bearing 150 degrees. Galantin's response was to snap out the order that put four diesels on the line and *Halibut,* trembling under the sudden surge of power, raced ahead with a bone in her teeth. Then Galantin, a New Yorker, wheeled around to his exec: "Guy, get down there and tell Conant to send a contact report!"

"What about the VHF watch, Captain?"

"Don't let 'em secure just yet," Galantin replied. "We need all the help we can get."

Gugliotta plunged down the hatch and seven long minutes evanesced in a welter of preparation. Another bomb concussion resounded through the hull, another puff of smoke. Then a steady succession of reports from the radio shack. *Halibut's* crew raced to battle stations, the alarm academic at this point. In the forward torpedo room, CTM James Soulis was already standing by ready to open outer doors on command.

Gugliotta returned at about the moment that seven pairs of glasses focused on heavy antiaircraft fire ahead.

"Message coded," he said tersely, moving to the New Yorker's side. "Transmitter warmed. *My God! Where the hell did that barrage come from?"*

"Been there waiting for us all the time," Galantin

chuckled: "Black and purple bursts above, white below—that's business, Mister!"

The exec ran a hand across his sweat-soaked chin. He stared for a moment at *Halibut's* knifing bow and wondered idly when Galantin was going to pull the plug. But his CO, a study in concentration, did nothing. The range came down inexorably and soon planes were seen flying through the puffballs of smoke. Time: five-thirty-nine. A radioman popped up on the ladder and reported that *Tuna* and *Haddock*, the two other members of the wolfpack, had been properly informed. Below, radar had a clear picture of the targets and the word flashed to the bridge:

"Captain! Range to targets 31,000 yards!"

Pete Galantin, squinting intently into the smoke, thought he saw the outline of battleship pagodas. Wheeling around to the grim-faced OOD, he snapped:

"Okay, Kendall, take 'er down! Let's get the bastards!"

The claxon blasts that followed this order brought a tidal wave of feet plummeting through the hatch. Luzon Strait quickly spilled noisily into empty ballast tanks and over wood-slotted decks as *Halibut*, fangs bared, rushed to the targets at top submerged speed.

Galantin breathed easier.

Removal of his sub from the surface materially enhanced her chances of closing without being detected by Jap radar. He took the con from the small, cramped tower, while in the control room below, a half-dozen officers converged on the chart table. Time, distance, bearings came into the sub's lexicon. Galantin brought *Halibut* to periscope depth. Rising into a crouch as the softly whirring 'scope moved up out of the well, he snapped down the handles and passed sighting information to Guy Gugliotta, official kibitzer, during the approach.

"Three of 'em! Escorts look like a *Yubari*-class cruiser and a destroyer. The can's been hit—"

"Captain, what about the BB?"

"Still coming down the track big as life! Sound —got anything?"

RM 2/c Donald Graham Bice sat tensely hunched over the handle of the sound recorder, slowly swinging the handle left and right. He said:

"Steady on reported bearings, Captain. Strong, solid contacts, sir."

Galantin wiped the sheen of perspiration gathering in the folds of his neck. "Good!" he grunted, stepping away from the periscope. "Okay, Guy— take a look. Remember everything you see."

The range closed, Galantin meanwhile jockeying the sub into attacking position 5,000 yards ahead of the target. More "Up 'Scope! Down 'Scope!" More long minutes slowly ticking off. The muted voice of the grim-faced J-1 talker at Galantin's elbow was heard keeping up a running commentary of the approach. In all compartments, men tuned their tension to the conning tower—aware that this was no ordinary target. In the control room, the dials of the torpedo data computer ground in the correct solution for the Jap BB, the primary target. Here stood Jim Conant, doubling in brass as TDC officer, and taking his bearings from Guy Gugliotta ... Then, from the conning tower: "Target should pass about 400 yards off our track, port side—open the outer doors!"

Forward, there was a decisive *thump* and *Halibut's* crew knew that the moment was at hand. Six Mark 18 electric torpedoes were ready; these were wakeless but slower jobs than conventional steam pickles —slower yet far more reliable. All fish were to be fired at five second intervals. *Halibut's* periscope broke water, and almost immediately there was a new urgency in her skipper's voice:

"Take 'er down—fast! *Fast!*"

"What's going on, Captain?"

"Escorts," Galantin pulled away, staring darkly at the exec. "Flashing lights on a yardarm blinker —they must have seen something. Let's sit a minute."

Halibut sat, holding her breath... waiting... all hands silently saying a prayer... until the New Yorker brought her back to periscope depth.

"Still there!" he whispered tersely. "Targets still coming!"

His voice took on a strange, incisive tone:

"Depth twenty feet, generated run 3,400 yards. Set for a 95 degree port track."

This was a shooting observation—a longer torpedo run than Pete Galantin had originally anticipated, but a better track to the target. Now the seconds fairly flew; in the forward torpedo room Soulis was standing by, hand on solenoid ready to fire manually in the event of a power failure; in control, Conant was urging softly that TDC had a correct solution. It was time. *Halibut* gathered herself like a coiled rattler and struck:

"Fire one! Fire two! Fire three! Fire four! Fire five! Fire six!" Then: *"Take 'er down fast! Rig for silent running—rig for depth charge!"*

Mark 18s spewed into Luzon Strait as Galantin, perspiration rolling down his cheeks, stood with stopwatch in hand timing the long run. None spoke, none breathed. The sea rushed into empty tubes forward and the submarine's bow slanted downward. But in the control room, diving officer Lieutenant John Hinchey was ready for this moment and the sub's trim was quickly restored.

Again silence. In the tower Pete Galantin's stopwatch ticked off long minutes... torpedoes running ... running ... there. Throughout the boat men wondered, prayed, listened, squeezed their eyes shut tight and rode with the fish. Then:

"Wrrangg! Wrrangg! Wrrangg! Wrrangg! Wrrangg!"

Loud, perfectly-timed explosions—five out of six—rocked the submarine, instantly followed by grotesque breaking up noises, air lines going crazy, underwater explosions! Galantin, all smiles as a subdued pandemonium broke loose in all compartments, listened to ecstatic phrases drifting up to the conning tower:

"The Old Man did it! He nailed the BB with five pickles!"

"Screws, Captain!" Bice intoned, leaning into his sound recorder. "Two sets—backing up and going ahead."

"Escorts picking up survivors," Galantin muttered. "Maybe if they keep it up, they'll forget about us."

He turned to a sailor.

"Get the book, Leo. Let's see if we can find the fruit of our labor—"

Sagging against a bulkhead, the New Yorker mopped his face. Here was mirrored the exhaustion, relief, elation, apprehension felt by the eighty-odd man crew. Where, he wondered, are those A/S measures? What the hell gives? These anxious thoughts took second place when the sailor returned with ONI 41-42—enemy identification book—and Galantin, with other officers who had seen the target, pored over the pictures until identifying the Jap as an *Ise* or *Yamashiro*-class battleship. Twenty hot minutes melted away: no charges. Nothing.

Halibut slowly planed to the surface and popped the hatch. It was dark now and off in the distance, the target was nothing but "a very large mound, no superstructure visible, strongly resembling the hull of a large capsizing ship." This description, unfortunately, was to stand for all time, as lookouts suddenly spotted gunflashes and lights on the horizon and Galantin ordered a chase.

However, only one item of particular significance occurred in the next sixty minutes: a spectacular explosion in the direction of the fleeing Jap escorts, "like a magazine blowing sky high.". Quite a sight, but *Halibut* never came close enough for a good look.

"By successive zigs to keep us astern," the New Yorker noted in his patrol report, "they managed to pull away . . ."

By now bone-weary and disgusted, Galantin broke off the chase, sent off his contact reports and headed about to his assigned area. Only one brief sequel remained to be played out that October 25, 1944. An hour later, at ten fifty-two a five-ship enemy task force steamed into the sub's area. Detected at 32,000 yards, another frantic chase ensued with the same dismal results. Galantin called it a night.

Round one of his epic tenth war patrol was over; round two—when the Japs *wouldn't* run—was coming up . . .

Even before Ignatius Joseph "Pete" Galantin— currently a rear admiral and director of the Navy's Special Projects program [Polaris]—assumed command, *Halibut* was a standout performer in the submarine war. Her first four patrols under Commander Royce H. Gross had given her a score of almost 23,000 tons of Jap shipping. Galantin, in replacing "Googy" Gross, had a large pair of shoes to fill.

Fresh from exec chores aboard the ill-fated *Sculpin*, and prior to that successive duty on the *R-11* and *S-24*, the affable, lanky New Yorker was chafing for a fight as top man aboard a fleet-boat. And he found one. On his first war patrol at *Halibut's* periscope, Galantin demonstrated the aggressive leadership inherent in high-scoring submariners: Silver Star for a downed freighter and a severely damaged aircraft carrier.

Halibut's crew of veterans now saw that they had a "hot skipper," a man who looked for trouble and generally found it. Into Jap-controlled waters sailed the sub on her next [sixth] patrol, hunting good targets, a long but rewarding hunt. Down went 9,000 tons of enemy shipping that run; a destroyer was damaged and a 150-ton sampan was riddled in a running gunfight. Second Silver Star from ComSubPac.

Next a couple of disappointing dry patrols when *Halibut* couldn't buy a hit ... Then finally that great day on the ninth patrol: pips all over the radar scope, a sneak-in undetected, *wrrangg*! Crackled ice. Some 13,000 tons damaged, 5,000 tons sunk. Galantin [Annapolis '33 and intercollegiate fencing champion] brought the flat fish home for his third Silver Star.

In Japan, the clans had gathered for the decisive Battle of Leyte and at the end of October, three enemy task forces converged on the Third and Seventh Fleets supporting the American landings. But operation *Sho* failed and *Halibut*, a member of one of the wolfpacks spaced out in Luzon Strait to nail strays, found them and flailed away.

Although the Japs were reluctant to admit *any* sinking, and never did acknowledge the big one of October 25, Galantin received credit for the sinking of the destroyer *Aitkisuki*—the escort which apparently blew sky high that fateful night.

Pete Galantin, of Hungarian parentage who would one day boss a fleet of missile-carrying atomic submarines, was on his way to submarine immortality and a Navy Cross. He had demonstrated *Halibut's* ability to dish it out in the first phase of the tenth war patrol. Now, nineteen days later, he would prove that she could take it as well.

November 14 at eleven forty-six *Halibut* was lying submerged in Bashi Channel, a convoy lane. Pete Galantin was sacked out after a long night on the bridge. The sub's air banks were full and her batteries charged. A patrol that had begun with *Halibut's* shaking a hot pair of dice, was nearing a routine if disappointing end. Then:

"Sir," the voice of the soundman clipped the silence of the conning tower. "Somebody's pinging."

Lieutenant John Hinchey lunged for the sweaty earphones proffered by the soundman. The handle of the recorder moved left, then right. Hinchey wheeled around to a sailor:

"Wake the captain! Sound contact!"

Seconds later, a sailor was racing down the narrow passage of the forward room into officer's country, rapping on the thirty-four-year-old captain's cabin. He repeated the conning tower's findings and Galantin, still in pajamas, raced into the control room and thundered up the ladder. After listening himself for a moment, Galantin ordered full submerged speed. The bearing was 154 degrees, loud and clear.

Then he returned to his cabin and tossed on his khakis.

At twelve twenty-two, *Halibut* was at periscope depth and Galantin was staring at the tops of a northbound convoy.

"Down 'scope!" he snapped, wheeling around to Gugliotta all smiles. "Business—that pinging is from a convoy. Battle stations!"

At twelve thirty two, another look. Galantin's voice was now tensely reeling off the periscope picture:

"One large, two smaller freighters. Three PC boats. Planes galore. Large bomber, old bi-plane over the far side of convoy. They're coming right to us."

The range closed still further and now Galantin was slowly swinging the periscope in a complete circle. Backing off, the CO eased away to let his executive officer have a look.

"Escorts are all on our side, Captain," Gugliotta grunted. "Possibly others. I get four freighters now. The big joker looks like table meat."

"Check. That's the tone I had in mind."

Twisting around to Bice, the skipper called tersely: "What's the poop, boy?"

"Three spitkits pinging, Captain. Approximately the same positions as before, sir."

Halibut bored in at top submerged speed as Galantin called for down 'scope. The minutes dragged. Then another observation, and in the control room the tracking party taking down the information relayed by Gugliotta.

"Primary target zig-zagging every four minutes," Galantin hissed. "Spitkits and planes proving heavy cover."

Finally, from the young skipper long minutes later:

· "This is a shooting observation. Range: 3,100 yards, 60 degrees starboard track—how's the set-up?"

From Conant: "Looks good, sir."

Outer torpedo doors thumped open, more minutes elapsing until TDC operator Conant grated:

"You can shoot any time, Captain!"

The picture in the periscope was that of the primary target: a large, modern freighter, with Jap PCs stacked up on the submarine's side of the convoy. Time: one-nineteen, nearly two hours since the original contact had been made. Motionless, his voice almost a whisper, Galantin spat out the fateful words:

"Fire one! Fire two! Fire three! Fire four!"

Halibut's 'scope dipped under and a long torpedo run—three minutes—began ticking off on the captain's stopwatch ... nothing. Galantin brought the lens out of water in time to focus again on the convoy. Suddenly the big freighter was making dense black smoke and dropping astern, but no ear-shattering *wrrangg* echoed through the boat. Only in the forward torpedo room was a single explosion felt and news of this was telephoned above. *Halibut* swung for stern shots at about the time Bice said:

"Range to escorts 2,000 yards, sir. Here they come!"

Halibut, belaying torpedo intentions, twisted about sharply and went deep rigged for silent running.

These were no defeated warships trying to escape the wrath of Third Fleet; these were ships and planes of a crack Jap A/S team charged with the protection of a convoy. Streaking in toward the submarine at this moment were aircraft equipped with *jikitanchiki*, the newest and latest electronic gimmick designed to finger marauding submarines. And finger it did. Even at two hundred feet and rigged for depth charge, *Halibut* now had the distinction of becoming the first American undersea boat to feel the sting of Japanese science.

"Escorts still closing," Bice reported. "Three sets of screws coming fast—"

Tensely silent sailors braced themselves against a conventional depth charging: a few energetically dumped cans and then, as Jap escorts were prone to do, an abrupt departure. But what ensued was not conventional, nor was the A/S team just another bunch of irate spitkits. At Galantin's elbow, a grim-faced J-1 talker suddenly noted that the forward torpedo room was reporting a loud, strange buzzing sound—something never heard before,- something weird and distinctly different than an erratic-run torpedo. Then: *"Clink-BLAM!"*

A moment later: *"Clink-BLAM! Clink-BLAM!"* There were close—too close for comfort. The thirty-four-year-old New Yorker grunted responsively: "Take 'er down to three hundred feet!"

Throughout the submarine light bulbs were popping, cork insulation was spraying out from sweaty bulkheads and overhead, and badly shaken sailors were trying vainly to catch loose gear that was suddenly falling onto a sharply canted deck. *Halibut* dug for the depths in a vain attempt to shake off her pursuers, but *jikitanchiki* was not to be eluded.

In after battery, bluejackets heard the buzzing

sound passing directly overhead—four times—approaching from starboard.

In the conning tower, Donald Graham Bice heard it on the sound gear as it circled the trapped submarine.

In the forward torpedo room, horrified sailors heard it clearly but couldn't distinguish the direction.

"Blam!"

The charge, right on, was without heralding click. It dished in the port side of the conning tower, admitting the sea, shattering instruments and gauges, and throwing the compartment into a hot wet darkness. Here, Pete Galantin and a half-dozen officers and men lay in a confused tangle of arms and legs, struggling to escape the inward flow of water.

"Secure the tower! All hands lay below!" he barked, while frantic crewmen scrambled down the ladder into the control room. Nobody was injured, and the badly shaken men complied with the order and continued their fight to save the boat from below. "Hinchey!" the future admiral addressed himself to the diving officer. "Take 'er down another fifty feet. Hard left rudder—"

"The forward torpedo room is taking water, Captain!" Chief of the boat David Lee Roberson streaked to Galantin's side.

"Do the best you can up there—check the damage in all compartments."

Then, remarkably, three minutes of freedom from *jikitanchiki* as Japanese airmen apparently lost the scent, for the ashcans stopped coming and *Halibut's* crew worked frantically in battle-lighted compartments to plug leaks and assess extensive damage suffered in the initial moments. In the forward torpedo room where a sound watch had somehow been resumed, a talker passed the word that now there were two escorts pinging on either quarter. The sub braced herself just as hammer blows suddenly

began raining down in accurate, frightening profusion: *"Blam! Blam! Blam!"*

The resounding concussion was hell itself. Three
dead-on charges tumbled sailors along the wet decks
and the bow came down sharply. *Halibut* plunged far
below her rated depth before a small knot of frightened men at her bow and stern planes could restore
trim. The worst of it was the damage, and this was
everywhere.

In the forward torpedo room, the deck plates were
dislodged and crewmen ended up in the bilges. The
skids, with their torpedoes, jumped a foot high and
sea valves immediately spun open. Water started
leaking through the escape trunk, bolts sheared off
and large wrinkles appeared in the pressure hull and
tank tops. The No. 1 air bank, after the last hammer, blew a stream of high pressure air into the
compartment and this wildly hissing sound, blend-
ing with the odors of hair tonic, shaving lotion, glyp-
tol and food, gave the impression that *Halibut* was
about to become another "overdue, presumed lost."

Here, air pressure built up to fifty pounds and
frantic crewmen believing that the boat was sinking
and that chlorine gas had begun leaking into the
battered room, sealed off the compartment. Word
of this came back by way of Roberson.

"Sir," the chief of the boat charged up to Galantin
in the control room, "forward torpedo's been secured.
That room's a mess."

"Anybody hurt—how bad is it?"

Roberson quickly told the sad story. Galantin
swiveled around to Gugliotta.

"Take over," he said. "I'm going forward."

In the battle-lighted passageway, the sweat-
soaked skipper saw a badly shaken bunch of sailors
beside the door to the torpedo room.

"How bad?" he asked Soulis, and the torpedoman
told him.

Roberson, meanwhile, had gone aft into the engine rooms. There was little damage here, curiously: vibration and a smoking No. 2 main generator, indicating burned pigtails and rings, but nothing else. But the chief of the boat found a vastly different story waiting for him in the other compartments: battery cells cracked; all bulkheads and partitions sprung or loosened from the hull; support for after port battery water tank loose; No. 2 periscope damaged; bow buoyancy tank cracked; tubes out of alignment; tilting motor and hydraulic pump out of alignment; all interior equipment—air conditioning, ice machine—finished; gyros knocked out; pit log damaged beyond repair; SD radar mast flooded; shafts noisy; all radio mast gear out or carried away.

In the forward room, Galantin was working in the tremendous heat with torpedomen trying to jack open the door to the torpedo room. Somehow the feat was accomplished and the pressure instantly dropped to twenty-eight pounds. Then the CO staggered back to the control room and took over again. The sight of sailors shoving rags into leaks, trying to plug water-gushing manifolds and gauges was staggering. Throughout the length of the submarine at this moment, frantically working sailors were talking to God. *Halibut*, a floating junk heap more dead than alive, waited grimly for the next charge to come down and send her off to eternity.

But the charge never came. Forward, sound heads were being trained manually, and a stunned, incredulous sailor blurted in a voice that was half-sobbing: *"The Japs are quitting! They're going away, Captain—screws going away!"*

At first, nobody believed it. Then the minutes ticked away and the ashcans didn't come down and the only sound above a human voice was that of water, leaking into the stricken submarine.

Galantin heard himself say softly, "Thank you, Sir!"

For a long time *Halibut* waited for the Jap escorts

to move well clear of the area, and in the battle-lighted control room a small knot of men watched the tall young skipper move to the side of the diving officer and say quietly:

"All right, Hinchley. Let's go upstairs—it's over."

Time. four forty-five, a three hour ride to hell and back, since the first depth charge . . .

When *Halibut* popped the hatch, an amazed inspection party found still more damage—the forward 4-inch gun had a breach cover smashed and punctured, and the chamber pushed to port. Periscopes were warped, one still operable. Then the beautiful music of the diesels again and crewmen, pinching their gooseflesh, stared numbly at the calm, bright waters of Bashi Channel and heard Pete Galantin tell the OOD:

"Wind 'em up, boy. This lady's due at the barn."

Westward she went, staggering with a peculiar pride and dignity that was to be remembered by the men of the submarine service.

In a while at Portsmouth Navy Yard, an amazed survey board would go over her from stem to stern and decree that her distinguished career was over. She would never return to sea . . . damage too extensive . . . scrap 'er.

A lanky, handsome rear admiral who now concerns himself with the operation of America's atomic submarines, Pete Galantin, can look back on that epochal tenth war patrol with immeasurable pride.

THE RESCUE OF ENSIGN GALVIN

OVER WOLEAI, deep in the Japanese-held Carolines, U.S. Navy carrier planes—fighters, bombers, torpedo planes—were working over enemy installations in a concerted daylight strike. Like frantic baitfish wheeling and diving on a school of hapless baitfish, hundreds of Task Force 58 aircraft literally were blowing Woleai to hell.

Two miles offshore, the submarine *Harder* was standing by on lifeguard assignment. Her mission: the rescue of downed aviators. On the sub's bridge, watching the giant air show, Lieutenant Commander Samuel D. Dealey, thirty-eight, squinted through a pair of binoculars at the south shore of the island. There, Japanese gunners were sporadically banging out a few rounds in token resistance.

The time: 0830 hours. The date: November 1, 1944.

In *Harder's* periscope shears, four sharp-eyed lookouts almost simultaneously spotted a point of smoke trailing from one of the fighters.

"One of 'em's hit, Captain!"

Sam Dealey swiveled around. Tall, deceptively calm, a Texan, the submarine skipper turned instantly to his executive officer, Lieutenant Frank Lynch:

"Check with Levin [communications officer]. See if anything's coming over that high freq radio!"

As Lynch turned and dropped down the conning tower ladder, Dealey passed the word to the engine rooms:

"All engines ahead flank! There's business out there!"

Then: "New course zero two zero! Let's roll!"

Coming around on bearing, *Harder* plunged through the bright, glassy seas toward the splashed plane, while Navy fighters suddenly peeled off from their attack and raced protectively overhead. In the radio shack, Lieutenant Ray Levin had succeeded a few moments before in establishing voice communications with a flight leader. The latter's message:

"Get on your hoss, sub. There's a fighter on fire and about to splash five miles north of the second island west of Woleai. He's bailing out now—"

Reported to the bridge, this message brought Dealey down to the shack in a rush.

In the control room, Frank Lynch was now laying out a new course based on the voice communication—computing distance to the pilot's estimated position. The exec shook his head darkly:

"He's a good three hours from us, Captain. I don't know..."

Then Levin was shouting from the radio shack: "The squadron leader says the zoomie is drifting with the wind toward a reef-bordered island—"

Dealey thumbed the intercom to the forward torpedo room:

"Get that rubber boat inflated forward room. Start curling your heaving line—there's business!"

Lynch grunted: "Sir, looks like there's some decent operating seas around there. Twenty fathoms or more. Chances are we can get in there and pick the guy up."

"Yeah," Dealey drawled acidly, "if those Jap guns on shore don't get the bastard first."

Dealey discreetly forgot to mention that *Harder* was about to become highly vulnerable too. If Jap aircraft ever caught her on the surface, that was it. The skipper said:

"Tell Sam Logan this zoomie's his baby. I want only volunteers, though. Have 'em briefed and standing by."

Then the Texan returned to the bridge. His exec cornered Lieutenant Sam Logan, the torpedo officer, coming back from the forward room.

"Your party, Sam," he said quietly, looking at the other for a long moment. "Skipper says for you to pick 'em carefully—only single men."

Logan sucked in his breath and tried to sound casual.

"Yes, sir," he nodded. "Will do."

Topside, Dealey and his bridge crew had a moment to watch the plastering being administered to Woleai. Bombs of all sizes rained down in profusion; buildings, oil dumps, radio station were lifted high in the air in a tidal wave of explosions. The entire island was covered with heavy clouds of black smoke, through which darting Navy aircraft could be seen. Nothing of value was left to the Japs on this morning of flaming death.

Dealey shifted his eyes to the forward deck. From the torpedo room, sailors were dragging aloft an inflatable yellow raft and placing it on deck. This meant that for the next few hours *Harder* was Zero bait—fair prey for any Jap plane that managed to ride out the Woleai storm. Dealey [Annapolis '30] liked this idea of staying surfaced about as much as he did a dished in tower, but neither he nor anybody else aboard spoke their private fears.

One of the hottest skippers in the sub service, the Texan particularly doted on down the throat shots in scoring his kills. One patrol run alone netted

Harder five Jap tin cans, only because of Dealey's insistence to twist around and stay up as long as possible and at the last minute to fire his bow tubes. A boat that made her name in a rush, commissioned only in December, 1943, Sam Dealey's sub was about to carve a unique niche in submarine history . . . the hard way.

Three hours melted in a welter of last minute detail. On deck was Sam Logan, cussing out his luck because in the search for volunteers [there were plenty of 'em], somebody had neglected to bring the paddles for the rubber boat. There was J. W. Thomason, SC 1/c, and Francis X. Ryan MoMM 1/c. Between the three of them, the business of squaring away for a particularly hazardous rescue was effected.

On the bridge, Sam Dealey's lookouts had finally spotted the pilot, roughly in the position described by the squadron leader: on the northwest tip of the second island to the west of Woleai.

"Battle stations," Dealey rasped. "Flood negative."

As the sub crew responded, *Harder* was flooded down and maneuvered into a spot about 1,500 yards off the beach. White water was breaking over the shoals barely twenty yards ahead of the bow. The fathometer had ceased to record.

"Nuts to this," Dealey told his OOD. "Let's back off and try another approach. Keep your eye on that flyboy. He looks beat."

He was. Ensign John R. Galvin, a member of Fighting Squadron Eight from *Bunker Hill* was not only exhausted, he was tired of dodging sporadic Jap fire from the beaches and he just didn't give a damn any more. Bullets or no, Galvin was out in plain daylight racing along the edge of the reef yelling to the submariners.

"That flyboy thinks 'we're leaving him to the

wolves," Lynch growled. "The poor bastard's going
to get himself shot like that—"

"*Maybe*," Dealey grimaced. "But not if our guys
get to him first. All engines back full—let's see if we
can get in there closer!"

Harder slowly rumbled astern throwing spume and
white water over her slender after section. Just the
sight of the submarine backing off was sufficient to
low bridge the flier. He screamed himself hoarse and
then, all at once, seemed to collapse of shock and
slowly sag down into the shallow water. More than
ever now, Dealey resolved to get the submarine
closer—and did. As *Harder* ploughed into coral heads
from a different angle, the three men forward tossed
the rubber boat over the side and climbed down the
limber holes after it.

"Let's go, you guys," Dealey thundered impor-
tantly. "Get that zoomie before he drowns himself!
Hit it!"

Logan, in charge of the rescue party, decided it
was impossible to get the boat in any way other than
towing and after a moment's deliberation the three
men jumped in. Pushing and towing against the
surge of a four-knot tide, they somehow forced the
boat toward the beach. Distance to the downed
pilot was a good 1,200 yards, painfully slow business.
Nor was the process of pushing the boat made easier
by the pull of the water against a line—a line payed
out from the sub to the boat in order to pull it back
once the beach had been reached.

Notwithstanding these drawbacks, the three men
struggled toward their objective. But now something
new was added: a torpedo-bomber zoomed over the
beach and dropped another rubber boat. Galvin, re-
covering somewhat, had thrown himself in and was
trying to paddle seaward against a tide toward his
rescuers. He was getting nowhere fast when the
rescue party reached a spot where they could stand
up.

"Stay here with the boat!" Logan ordered Thomason. "Ryan and I'll get that guy——"

Then the lieutenant and the motor mack stumbled off in the direction of the zoomie, half-wading, half-swimming. Mauled by the booming surf and chafed against the sharp coral, thirty endless minutes elapsed before the two men reached the aviator. His raft had drifted in the tide, with the result that the last few minutes of the impossible rescue was achieved by swimming. Galvin, meanwhile, had pooped out again and was doubled over in his rubber raft only vaguely conscious. But when he saw the two submariners something apparently registered.

He croaked weakly: "Thank God! I never thought you people would make it here——"

"Neither did we," the sub's torpedo officer quipped. "Ryan, hold onto that rubber boat—keep 'er steady. Zoomie, you grab my shoulders and swing overboard. Snap it up, boy!"

The pilot complied. "Ensign John R. Galvin. *Bunker Hill*," he grunted as the surge of the tide tore at his body. "I didn't think a lousy ensign rated this treatment——"

"Thank the man over there," Ryan snapped. "The guy who runs the submarine."

The three men inched their way along the surf toward Thomason, who was fighting the surf's pull and trying hard to hold the boat in the same instant. It was work that came extremely hard.

And on the *Harder*, Commander Sam Dealey was having his share of troubles too. All four engines were on the line and he was trying to keep the bow into the reef, to keep from betting broadsides. This little trick was complicated somewhat by Jap sniper fire from the island, plus a new arrival on the frantic scene: a float plane from one of the Task Force 58 cruisers had come to Woleai to observe American marksmanship. Seeing the drama take place, the float plane pilot wanted to help and he inadvertently ran over the tow line and cut it.

To complicate things further, the surf was too much for Galvin and he promptly keeled over. This necessitated getting the free raft again and Logan and Ryan pushing him in. With this done, the two submariners again fought their way toward Thomason.

The next result of the newly added chaos was that the rescue party—all of it—was stranded. And more Jap bullets were *thwumping* into the surf around them.

Sam Dealey's Irish temper took over. Wheeling around to his exec, Frank Lynch, he snapped:

"I'll keep this goddam bucket right here. Now you go below and get me another volunteer on the double."

As the exec double-timed it down the conning tower hatch, more lead began whizzing around the superstructure. Dealey ordered lookouts below for their own protection, then slammed *Harder* fast into the reef. In a moment, up came Lynch with Freeman Paquet, Jr., GM 1/c, through the forward hatch. The latter, as rough a bluejacket as they came, grabbed the bitter end of a line in his left fist and dove overboard. Dealey shoved his head down toward the tower hatch:

"Pass the word! Tell those goddamn planes to keep clear—they're fouling up things here!"

But if this word was ever relayed by the radio shack, it was never acknowledged. Now, more than ever, planes finished with their work on Woleai, hovered above the 'rescue party' in an effort to provide air cover for Zeros.

This was fine in the overall, but it did precious little where sniping was concerned. Jap bullets kept pelting in and around them and, although nobody was actually hit, just the sight alone of that tufting water was frightening beyond words.

"Stay down!" Logan shouted. "Just stick enough of you out of the water to breathe!"

"I don't need any instructions, Mister Logan," the half-drowned, coral-cut Ryan retorted. *"I'm down, believe me!"*

Slowly, steadily, the two submariners towing the rubber boat with unconscious Galvin aboard neared Thomason. The latter released his hold on *Harder's* boat and plunged through the surf toward the others to bear a hand.

Harder, only about 500 yards offshore throughout the drama, maneuvered violently to hold her place against the reef. Those 500 yards seemed to the men in the water more like five miles. Pacquet, swimming with the line, was hidden to them by the breaking surf. All they could see in addition to sub, planes and tufting water, was the lugubrious picture of three half-drowned submariners about to meet their Maker face to face. Then, abruptly, Pacquet's body shot through the breakers and was tumbling in the wash almost at their feet.

He still had the line in his fist.

Ryan, acting on his own, plummeted into the white water to grab the gunner's mate before the tide picked him up and carried him back out.

Now there were five little Indians on the beach and the sub skipper was hollering through a megaphone to the knot of men on the foredeck: "When they get that line secured, haul easy! *Easy*, goddamnit—those Japs ain't about to stay put all day!"

Nor were they; but with air cover practically blanketing the area no Zeros were about to come too close, either. To the men in the water and those exposed on the sub's deck, however, exposure to enemy shore fire and the potential air threat was more than enough. They made fast Pacquet's line and waved to *Harder* to haul away.

Ray Levin, the comm officer, poked his head out of the tower: "Captain," he said, "Those planes say they've only got fuel for a little while. How much longer?"

"Beats me," Dealey grimaced. "God only knows the way things are going."

"What do I tell 'em?"

"Tell 'em we're doing our best," the sub skipper answered truthfully. "Tell 'em we're staying to see this job through. Besides, my men are on that coral spit and I'm staying until they're all back!"

"Yes, sir!" Levin grinned. "Yes, sir!"

On the beach, the four *Harder* sailors had secured the line to the rubber boat and were swimming with it through the breakers.

This line was attached on the other end to a dozen submariners, hauling it slowly hand over hand. But now, as the rescue party cleared the last line of breakers, Jap gunners ashore seemed to double their efforts for a kill. Bullets spattered among them like rain, so that only a desperate need for air drove them up for a moment.

The men swam and pulled, and inside the rubber boat the again vaguely conscious Ensign John R. Galvin flattened out against the possibility of one of the bullets hitting the craft. None did. The incredible last minutes of the rescue came off without a hitch as the boat brushed up against the submarine and exhausted men climbed up on limber holes. From this point, helping hands brought them aboard. Galvin was taken below to sickbay, his ordeal over.

"All engines back full!" Dealey barked. Then, a moment later: "Left full rudder! All ahead flank!"

Two Navy Crosses [Dealey and Logan] came out of the epic saga of a lifeguard mission; also three Silver Stars for the enlisted men. But the accolades weren't over quite yet: Pacific Boss Chester W. Nimitz, speaking from Pearl Harbor, added his own personal laurel ... "The Commander in Chief of the Pacific Fleet considers the performance of the commanding officer, the officers and the crew of the USS

Harder one of the outstanding rescue feats accomplished to date ... in keeping with the highest traditions of the entire submarine force ..."

John R. Galvin heartily agreed.

NIGHT OF THE KONGO

IN THE DARKENED conning tower of the submarine *Sealion II*, prowling the East China Sea on war patrol, the yellow blob of light flickering at the extreme upper right corner of the radar set puzzled Radioman 1/c Jim Mathias. The pip was too big for a Jap convoy, too distant for the coast of Formosa.

"Something's wrong with this JC set, Lieutenant Bates!" the sailor growled into the hole. "I keep getting land."

Instantly, Joe Bates climbed down from the black, overcast topside. Squeezing into the tight knot of submariners standing their watches in the conning tower, the OOD squinted long moments at the strange impulse before asking the radioman if the set otherwise checked out. Land, Bates said, was forty miles away.

"Yes, sir, Lieutenant," Mathias nodded vigorously. "Every once in a while this bugger shows me ghosts. But not tonight."

"Check it out once more."

Mathias complied, methodically, taking a screw driver to the azimuth scale and then pulling the antenna. After another moment, he pulled the picture tube and jammed it on the test meter. Nothing. Finally the set was reassembled and warmed, but

146

as before the pip was still there holding its own. Bates shrugged. Then swiveling around to the messenger of the watch, a signalman striker, he snapped:

"Better wake the captain, Ski. Maybe he can figure it out."

Nodding curtly, the sailor slid down the ladder and hurried forward. In his cabin, Commander Eli T. Reich was sleeping off a hard day at the periscope. A rugged, good looking New Yorker [P.S. 69] *Sealion II*'s thirty-four-year-old skipper was among those charged with hunting down Jap warships fleeing from Leyte Gulf. Reich's eyes were open on the messenger's first rap.

"What's up?"

"Lieutenant Bates wants you in the tower, Captain. Funny pip up there. Looks like Formosa, sir."

"Right there."

Bounding out of the sack, Reich, still in pajamas, sprinted aft into the control room and grabbed the ladder. In a few seconds he was staring at the distant yellow impulse and asking himself *how the hell can this be? Should the coast come up at these ranges?* Reich thundered up the ladder to the bridge where Bates was waiting.

"What do you think, Captain?"

"Beats me. No Jap convoy ever looked like that. It has to be the coast—"

The two men stared off in the general direction of the contact. In the shears, four lookouts were silent. Reich, freezing in only pajamas, twisted around to the ladder. But he stopped dead as the voice of Radioman Baker grated incisively through the hole:

"*Two targets of battleship proportions and two large cruiser-size! Course 060! Speed 16 knots! Not zigging!*"

The New Yorker, grinning from ear to ear, dropped like a stone into the tower and leaped toward Mathias, surrounded by the entire watch section and pointing at the impulse. Reich slammed the bluejacket's back elatedly.

"Stick with it!" he roared. "Keep me posted!"

Then he scrambled down the ladder and raced to his cabin, there to slip into khakis and splash a handful of water on his face. Elsewhere in the boat, even before battle stations officially sent the crew into action, the officers of the plotting party converged on the control room with charts and dividers. Scuttlebutt surged through the tiny compartments of the submarine like a plague ... *the Old Man's chasing a big one ... the whole goddamned Jap fleet ... what the hell are we waiting for—let's go ..!*

As the general alarm sounded and speed was upped to flank on four mains, *Sealion II's* skipper returned to the bridge. Bates had twisted her onto an end-around course, a course designed to have the sub first catch up with the convoy and then grayhound ahead into attack position. Nice theory, but a tall, tall order.

"Code a contact report to ComSubPac," Reich told the OOD, who was also the submarine's communications officer, "Tell him we're chasing the jackpot. Distance of target at least forty miles. Amplifier follows."

"Yes, sir!" Bates beamed. Relinquishing the deck to Lieutenant Jim Bryant, the exec, who'd arrived topsides with the sounding of the gong, Bates quickly went below to the wardroom and his coding board.

In the shack, the chief radioman was grinding the transmitter to full peak load. In the periscope shears, the four lookouts were straining against a visibility of 1,500 yards. On the bridge, the urgent throbbing of the diesels pounding up through the soles of sandals spelled out the precise meaning of this fateful night—attack.

"Jim," Reich wheeled around to his exec. "Lay below and tell Hagen [Lieutenant jg Harold Hagen, the engineer] to wind those goddamned rheostats.

And check the maneuvering room while you're there
—*I need knots!*"

In silent compliance, the exec plummeted through
the hatch and raced aft. Reich remained on deck a
few minutes longer, going over in his mind the impossible mission he'd tackled. Radar *alone* would
provide the sub with eyes and Reich, like any other
experienced underseas veteran, didn't especially thrill
to the idea of an all-electronic approach. Too much
could happen...a picture tube...a condenser...
some lousy little twist of the dials inadvertently...
a great sea busting over the bridge and deluging the
radar recorder in the tower...or simply a Jap admiral deciding to zigzag onto a new track which
would put *Sealion II* too far off the base course for
an intercept.

Eli Reich braced himself for the worst.

Lieutenant Clayton Brelsford, diving officer, poked
his head through the hatch. To Bryant he said formally: "Request permission to come to the bridge,
sir—"

"Permission granted," the exec snapped.

Reich, hearing the diving officer's voice, wheeled.
"You're a mind reader, boy," he said evenly. "I
was on my way down to tell you to pump everything.
I want this bucket dry and moving."

"Negative's been blown, Captain," the diving officer said. "And the six hundred pound manifold's on
the line right now. Anything else?"

"Not at the moment." Then Reich added: "Did
Hagen tell you what he's getting since we upped to
flank?"

"Twenty-one, Captain. He said the rheos are so
wound up, they'll probably begin sparking any minute—"

"That's a crock of stuff!" Reich grinned. "That
guy's always worrying about something!"

Two minutes later, Bates returned to the bridge.
The contact report to ComSubPac had been trans-

mitted. Reich said good, then turned to stare into a gradually rising sea. One of the lookouts was cursing the lousy visibility. Reich thought of the enlisted man, and of all his men wondering again how it would all come out in the end. He wondered about the effect of the contact on Vice-Admiral Charles N. Lockwood, the father confessor of the submarine force. The three-star was doubtless bouncing out of bed and rushing down to his headquarters in the Pearl Navy Yard.

Reich thought about the odds. Not good, really, all things considered. He thought, too, of his submarine's reliance exclusively upon radar. And that was something else that brought nagging doubts. He turned to the exec before doubling back on the radar recorder.

"Jim," he said softly. "I think we've got a chance —a good chance. I'm going to take a turn around the boat."

The exec nodded.

Reich went below.

In the conning tower, standing beside the operator and Lieutenant [jg] Dan Brooks, the submarine skipper watched the flickering yellow blob for a long moment. Mathias offered:

"Every once in a while that pip breaks up, but you can't tell a damned thing yet."

"What was your last range?"

"Twenty miles, sir."

"Convoy composition should be clear at 0100, Captain," Brooks said. "We're five knots ahead of them and gaining all the time—"

Reich nodded and took a step backward. In the control room, the plotting party was hard at work. Here, without saying much, he checked the calculations and made a few of his own. He thumbed the intercom to the bridge.

"Jim, everything checks out okay. We've got this convoy cold turkey if he doesn't zig—"

Then the New Yorker made a quick tour, starting forward at the torpedo room where a chief was checking out the solenoid system in preparation to opening outer doors. Here, as everywhere, the crew asked essentially the same questions: *When do we shoot, Captain? Targets still up there, sir? How big do you figure the bastards are, sir? Is the radar set still perking, sir?*

In the engineering spaces where the temperature now stood at nearly 100, the chief was shaking his head sadly and shouting a warning ... disaster, sparking, a brush burnout, vibration ... Reich, in the crew's quarters when Bates streamed back waving a decoded message from ComSubPac, read Lockwood's encouraging reply with one hand gripping an overhead railing. His sub, pitching and creaking down to her keel, was fighting head seas and rising winds—phenomena that could end this chase in a blank.

By now, Reich realized, his sub should actually be flanking the enemy task force and going ahead on the end-around. And the picture on the screen should be up too, detailed, exact for firing bearings. He glanced at his watch: 0200, two hours since Mathias first noticed the pip. *What the hell gives up there?* he growled in his mind. Black thoughts crowded his mind, blacker with every step toward the control room. But then, abruptly, the excited voice of the radar officer was booming over the intercom:

"Captain to the tower! Captain to the tower!"

And Eli Thomas Reich came running ...

While the memorable November 21, 1944 would unquestionably have some bearing on the selection of the Navy's future Assistant Chief, Surface Missile Systems, rank of Rear Admiral, Reich's combat days had actually begun long before in the Philippines.

At Cavite Navy Yard when Jap bombers turned

that area into smoking shambles, Reich, a lieutenant, was attached to the first *Sealion* in the capacity of assistant engineering officer. He was ashore in the Yard when enemy planes flew over and dropped a stick on his submarine, a veteran undersea boat of the Asiatic squadron.

When the smoke cleared, *Sealion* was ripped apart and settling fast in the shallow waters of Manchina Wharf—the first American sub casualty of World War II. Fifteen days later, when the Navy abandoned the area, three charges were set off in *Sealion's* twisted wreckage and an unhappy scuttling was thus complete.

Few cases of poetic justice rival that of Eli Thomas Reich, the New York boy who was destined for Silent Service immortality. Immediately after *Sealion* ceased to exist, he moved over to the staff of Commander Submarines, Asiatic Fleet, to serve briefly on Bataan until the evacuation of that hotly contested station. Here, "in recognition of service" during the worst of that fighting Reich earned an Army Distinguished Unit Badge, one of the few Navy men to receive the accolade.

Escaping from Corregidor and Bataan aboard the submarine *Stingray*, Reich served on board as engineer and exec until September, 1942, when he was detached in connection with the fitting out and commissioning of the *Lapon*. Then came welcome orders—back to the States for the fitting out and commissioning of the second *Sealion*, his own command.

But it wasn't until March 8, 1944 that Reich's commission pennant was broken from the yard of this vessel and she proudly steamed off to the war in the Pacific. After topping off at Midway, Reich took *Sealion II* into a hot zone for a little torpedo retribution: Navy Cross for that first patrol, four enemy ships for a total of 19,600 tons. A good blooding.

Then, war patrol two, and this capable career

officer who was shaking an enviably hot set of dice, tossed out another seven: Navy Cross for a 2,300 ton destroyer, two large tankers and three large transports for a total of 51,700 tons. It was on this slam-bang sortie into enemy waters that Reich pickled, and rescued, fifty-four British and Aussie POWs from one of his sunken targets.

Thus affairs stood when the good-looking, rugged New Yorker came back to the barn for a torpedo reload and a long drink of fuel oil. The dice—still incredibly hot, and Eli Thomas Reich was of no mind to miss the third roll.

Out of R-boats, destroyers and a battleship [*Texas*], the kid from Newton High [Annapolis '35] who'd joined "out of a love of adventure and a desire to serve" was already something of a legend when ComSubPac sent him troubleshooting in the wake of the enemy's disaster at Leyte Gulf. Admiral Kurita's Second Fleet was fleeing down Formosa Straits— destroyers, cruisers, battlewagons all seeking sanctuary in the IJN's moment of extremis.

This was where Eli Thomas Reich, thirty-four, came in ... his third war patrol, and one which successive generations of U. S. submariners would study from many angles—tactical and poetic—found him directly in the track of Kurita's van.

Strictly a radar chase in the early phase of the fateful November 21st, as *Sealion II* was closing an impossible range and doing her end-around act, Reich was in the conning tower squinting at a wondrous picture a few moments after an urgent summons from the officer in charge of this station. The sea, wild and fighting the submarine every foot of the way, was no deterrent to Reich's ecstasy when the picture finally unfolded.

"That's it, Captain!" Dan Brooks told him, standing away from the scope. "Destroyers, cruisers, battlewagons—we're in!"

Reich was not so sure.

Staring at the screen, *Sealion's* skipper noted a perceptible change in the original pip. Now, two hours after the chase had begun, the impulse had broken up into two distinct formations and the size of each individual impulse indicated—to a trained observer—an enemy task force, destroyers flanking battleships and cruisers. It was a sight never to be forgotten, and crewmen and officers of the bridge-conning tower crew ganged around the screen oohing and aahing.

"Message from ComSubPac, Captain," Bates pounded up from the shack, waving Lockwood's second reaction to the contact report.

Swiftly Reich glanced at the decoded Urgent:

"HANG ON X WE ARE ALL PULLING FOR YOU ELI X."

"Any reply, sir?"

"Not yet," Reich replied hesitantly. "Let's see what develops with our picture."

Bates nodded and went below to tell radio to secure. Reich, swiveling back to *Sealion's* plunging bow, silently cursed the opaqueness. On the bridge with the skipper were exec Jim Bryant, the OOD Francis Holt, a jg, and Lieutenant Commander Charles Putnam, the PCO [Prospective Commanding Officer], who would be Reich's successor after this patrol. In the periscope shears about them were four lookouts. At 0246, after incessant trips to the radar recorder in the tower, a sailor suddenly growled:

"Object bearing broad on the starboard bow, sir!"

Binoculars snapped up to grim faces pressing hard against the curtain of black. Then, from Reich:

"Got it! Looks like a can—that jibes with the picture radar is getting! The can's ahead of a BB!"

Bryant stared wordlessly at his commanding officer, now wheeling around and calling into the tower for the telephone talker to tell forward room to standby. A moment later, Reich was back on his feet softly spewing orders to his exec. This was the plan: *Sealion II* would fire six electric fish from the forward tubes and, time permitting, would spin about and let fly with the four after jobs. The target was the BB behind the can. Next Reich passed the word for Bates to code his amplifying report, stating task force composition and the fact that he was nearing firing position. The submarine, taking white water over her plunging bow, now raced ahead as the word flashed down to open the outer doors.

"Still got the can?" Reich snapped at the lookout.

"Negative, Captain," came the grim reply, reflecting what amounted to utter misery. *"Negative!"*

"Search around—keep searching!"

Reich, dripping salt spray with sweat spanking down his foul weather gear, plunged into the conning tower and raced to the recorder. He was ahead of the Japanese task force. His torpedoes would run along a 70 degree track. He was 1,800 yards ahead of the nearest destroyer, presumably the ship his lookout had seen, and the target was riding dead astern.

"Set forward for eight feet. Set after for ten. Generated run 3,000 yards. Standby!" he grated.

Time: 0256.

In the control room, the plotting party reacted with swift adjustments as the dials of the torpedo data computer whirled in the correct solution. In all the compartments, men waited, breath in short sharp gulps. In the forward torpedo room, a chief clasped the headphones connecting him with the tower in a tight, icy grip. Beside him a white-faced telephone talker pressed the button and hissed:

"Forward room standing by—"

Reich sucked in his breath as a voice below barked the order for all engines to stop.

The destroyer was passing Sealion II on the screen and the impulse of the BB was coming up. This was the moment, now—now.

"Fire one!....Fire two!...Fire three!...Fire four!...Fire five!...Fire six!"

From the forward room to the hot cramped tower: "All fish fired electrically...all fish away, sir!"

"Right full rudder," snapped Reich. The sub pirouetted around toward the second column. *"Fire seven!...Fire eight!...Fire nine!...Fire ten!..."*

Reich's eyes darted downward to his stop watch, the deed done, the electrics running...clawing through the turbulence...the screen pregnant with flickering yellow blobs of light. And in his mind a long prayer, the same prayer on the lips of eighty men. On the darkened bridge where Bryant, Holt and Putnam strained along with the lookouts on the precise bearing, there was only silence. Loud, long silence lasting exactly sixty eternity-filled seconds. Then:

Wrrangg! Wrrangg! Wrrangg!

On the bridge seven pairs of eyes widened incredulously as a tremendous sheet of flame turned the blackness to bright yellow-orange. In the tower, all hands blinked in amazement and disbelief as a smear of yellow flashed up from the angle of impulse. Topside men were shouting ecstatically but Eli Thomas Reich heard none of it clearly. He was shouting furiously:

"Course two seven zero—flank speed! Let's get the hell out of here!"

Sealion II, clawing her way against head seas, struggled to clear the area as Japanese destroyers combed the spot and loud, repeated explosions thundered in the direction of the Jap task force. Across the sea, the smear of light burned itself out and those in the submarine could only guess about the outcome. They had pickled something—what? Reich moved out for a reload and then whipped around again, speed decreased by head seas and sparking motors.

Reich moved onto the bridge, wondering how badly

damaged were his targets. Then, for two hours, as the Japs opened wide and he clawed for another end-around, came word from Brooks on the radar recorder:

"Column is breaking up, dispersing, Captain!"

"Range?"

"Seventeen thousand yards, sir—"

"Stand by all tubes. We're almost set here."

The submarine closed, speed falling, seas busting over the peak deluging the men on the bridge. Another fifteen minutes. More seas shaking the boat like a terrier with a rat in its jaws. Eighty men wondering, praying, frantically asking compartment talkers to check with the tower—was the target still there?

On the bridge the silent knot of officers huddled together, gripping stanchions to keep from falling, watching the monstrous seas and the blackness beyond. Then Eli Thomas Reich and his officers and the lookouts above saw a wondrous sight on the stygian ocean. Suddenly there was a flash—greater than before—and one clap of thunder—greater than before—and then the night turned to brightest noon off in the direction of the targets.

"Something's happened up here!" Reich boomed into the tube. There was a long ten second pause. Then the skipper's voice again: *"My God, our damaged battleship just blew up!"*

The light smeared over the horizon, framing the milling task force—battleship no longer in sight.

"All engines ahead flank! New course zero zero zero!"

But the chase of the enemy task force availed nothing except more green seas busting aqueous bombs. Throughout the submarine weary men ripped loose an assortment of wild, ecstatic cheers.

One battleship! Scratch one battleship! And a destroyer definitely hit, maybe sinking!

Reich and company reluctantly broke off the chase

and turned for the barn. The weather, fast developing into a tropical storm, wrote finis to an epic chase. It was over and *Sealion II* was still in one piece, tired but happy.

In Pearl Harbor, Reich received his third Navy Cross and there learned the identity of his target: *Kongo,* 31,000 tons! In the same shattering attack, destroyer *Urakaze* was put out of action. Presidential Unit Citation for a fighting submarine. Then rest camp and a two-week hiatus in the torpedo war against the dying Empire. His patrols were all behind him forever.

The sinking of the *Kongo,* the *only* Japanese battleship acknowledged as a casualty of the war, catapulted the New Yorker into submarine limelight which has never dimmed. Others had fired pickles and unquestionably dented enemy BBs, but Eli Thomas Reich was the only skipper to have his claim recognized...a case in point for the gods of vengeance.

THE SINKING
OF JAPAN'S BIGGEST CARRIER

PRECISELY at 8:48 P.M., November 28, 1944, the American submarine *Archerfish* was patrolling along the western edges of Sagami Nada—Tokyo Bay. Two diesels were on the line, and air banks and batteries were under charge. It was the seventeenth day of the submarine's fifth war patrol, and there was nothing exciting or extraordinary about it until the moment that RM 1/c James Laird, at radar, flipped his recorded scale to long range. A split second later, the sailor blinked incredulously: *five* pips—one of them as big as an island—had entered the omniscient radar beam!

"Mister Andrews!" Laird blurted. "Take a look."

Lieutenant John Andrews, the officer of the deck, swiveled sharply. Then he did a large size doubletake and hit the intercom:

"Captain to the bridge! Radar contact!"

In the wardroom where Lieutenant Commander Joe Enright and his exec, Lieutenant Zygmunt ["Bobo"] Bobcznski, were hunched over charts and coffee, the summary rasp of the squawk box was like a clap of thunder. Both men jumped up, raced into the companionway, hurtling into the control room and onto the thin steel ladder to the conning tower. Seconds later, the periscope was out of the well and Enright was squinting hard into the rubber-mounted peepsight.

"Too far to see anything," he snapped. He lurched over to the radar operator. "Got a range yet, Laird?"

"Yes, sir, Captain—easy 17,000 yards!"

Then Enright ducked lower, staring at the five juicy impulses. The targets were racing ahead of him, zigzagging. That meant a stern chase—impossible, maybe. And it meant running around the target—and end-around—in order to get into proper firing position: Time, distance, relative speeds, target angles, base course of target—all this and more flooded through Joe Enright's nimble brain in those initial seconds.

"Got speed and base course yet?"

"Yes, sir. Speed is twenty knots. Base course 240 degrees."

Enright grimaced. *Archerfish's* best was nineteen knots, more maybe if all the rheostats were pushed to their limits and somebody tossed over the five-inch deck gun. In the pit of the COs stomach was a palpitating kettledrum: *could anything catch up with those five pips now?* But his decision had already been reached even before these negative factors occurred: *chase!*

"Mister Andrews, sound battle stations," he snapped. "Send Cousins and Crosby up here on the double. All engines ahead flank—let's roll!"

Seconds later, *Archerfish* heeled around on a chase course and her four big diesels roared throatily. It was the beginning of a long night . . . and one which eighty-one submariners would never forget.

How could they? The biggest thing they'd gotten to date was the lead freighter of a five-ship convoy. Here and there a few sampans off Formosa, but nothing with meat on it. But such is the way of war—no man knows when Fate is about to put him in touch with a jackpot—or more properly, have him chasing one . . .

When Lieutenants Gordon Crosby and Rom Cousins, communications and engineering officers, respectively, appeared in the darkened conning tower, Joe Enright had specific orders for them both:

"Get this and get it straight," he stared hard at the engineer. "We're onto something big—damned big. I don't know exactly what it is, but the sonuvabitch is as big as an island. I want everything you can give me, Rom, and I want it now. Get going!"

To Crosby he said: "Code a message to ComSub-Pac. Tell him speed of target, base course and that we're chasing on a long end-around. Tell him I don't think we've got a snowball's chance in hell, but the bloody chase is on—"

The two officers disappeared below in a rush, and then Impossible Odds Enright hung around a few seconds more, checking radar, and went below. The plotting party was stationed at the control room table. Bobo Bobczynski was serving as assistant approach officer. The TDC [Torpedo Data Computer] was manned. Officers crouched around the charts with dividers and stop watches, noting times and distances and relative speeds.

Enright moved over to the diving stand where the Chief of the Boat Ed Brill was stationed. *Archerfish,* it seemed to the skipper, wasn't nearly picking up her heels yet and he didn't like it.

"Tell Mister Andrews to give her a five minute blow [blow safety and negative]—she's still dragging!"

"Yes, sir, Captain!" the enlisted whip nodded and he whirled around and lunged for the ladder.

Throughout the submarine, officers and enlisted men couldn't resist the temptation to speculate. A *battleship?*

Hadn't the radar watch reported the target as big as an island? Must be a battleship, they concluded, or else a damned big carrier? But nobody seriously considered the latter. Carriers were *the jackpot,* and jackpots were always elusive, in addition to being heavily screened by destroyers. Nevertheless, an electric tension surged through all the dimly lit compartments. Whatever it is, crewmen thought, it's damned big and worth chasing. But at the impossible range nobody was willing to believe that *Archerfish* would ever throw a spread of torpedoes this night.

Deep within his heart, Joe Enright knew he didn't stand a chance of catching the enemy task force— not unless that task force suddenly zigzagged along a *different* base course, and one which obviously brought the hunter and hunted closer together. Not much to go on, but enough for a longshot player who wanted to leave his trademark on the Japanese Empire forever.

A few moments later, the CO was back in the conning tower anxiously peering over the shoulders of his radarman at the 'scope. There seemed to be no appreciable difference in yardage yet. He hit the intercom hard:

"Rom, this is the captain. What the hell are you people making back there?"

"Pit log registers 19.5 knots, sir."

"Not enough. Do something different—give me some goddamn knots!"

The whining screech of the remote control governor told him that *Archerfish*'s ballast tanks were bone dry. So much for that. What else could he do? He stalked around the battle-lighted control room muttering to himself.

Below, in the radio shack, Lieutenant Gordon Crosby had finished ciphering *Archerfish*'s message to ComSubPac [Commander Submarines Pacific] and handed it to the first class on watch.

"Here," he snapped. "Wind that sonuvabitch and start pounding!"

"Your slightest wish," grinned the swabby, "is my command, sir."

"Damned right it is!" snarled Crosby, and he tossed down the message.

Two hours later, Crosby would code another message and this one—the amplifier—would have the effect of 100,000 volts at Pearl Harbor.

For two hours later, Enright was grousing around the chart room table when the word suddenly came down from the conning tower that the target had changed course to two six zero. Lieutenant Dave Bunting, the TDC operator, twisted the dials of his instrument and his mouth dropped open. At the same moment, Bobczynski looked up from his dividers and grinned.

"Captain, I think we got it made!"

Enright didn't wait for clarification. He grabbed the ladder and shot up to the tower, peering over the sweat-ridden back of the operator. Then he punched up through the hole and bulled his way to the spray shield. Only Lieutenant [jg] James Diggs, a quartermaster and a J-1 [telephone] talker stood on the bridge. But above, in the periscope shears were five alert lookouts. Then, from the tower:

"Target! Bearing two seven zero, Captain!"

"Range?"

"12,500 yards, sir."

"Keep me informed."

California-born Joe Enright, thirty-six, danced in his heart. *The ever-zigging Japanese had unwittingly cut the range down by their continual gyrations! But not far enough.* He whirled around to the lookouts, and his words were clipped and intended for all on that darkened bridge:

"Okay, you men. What we're chasing should show up on the horizon soon. Keep your eyes open. First man who makes the sighting gets an extra week's liberty—"

The incentive wasn't needed. Whatever Joe Enright wanted, so did his crew. Time dragged for all

of them ... fifteen ... twenty ... twenty-two minutes
elapsed as eight pairs of eyes squinted into the black
wash of the Pacific.

And then: "Captain! I think I see 'em!"

Simultaneously from the tower: "The target has
zigged toward us again, Captain!"

The bridge crew pressed hard into their night
glasses, scanning across miles of open ocean on a
black night where horizon and sea were one. And then
the same lookout called down:

"I can't tell how many, Captain, but they're just
forward of the port beam—"

"It looks to me like a bunch of cans around an aircraft carrier! Send the comm officer up here on the
double!"

Lieutenant Crosby scampered up to the bridge
immediately, pad and pencil ready. "Take this down,"
Archerfish's longshot CO grunted. *"From Archerfish
to ComSubPac and all subs in empire area. Pursuing
large aircraft carrier, four destroyers.* That's it,
Gordon—get it off!"

The communication officer wheeled around and
plunged through the hole. A few moments later, he
was stripping the message and dashing back to the
shack. The swabby on the key didn't waste time on
social preliminaries. He just sent:

"Urgent from Archerfish! *Urgent from* Archerfish
—answer!"

But Pearl Harbor went on with its routine traffic
until the submarine's radioman broke in with *"Really*
urgent!"

Then came the immediate signal "K"—the desig-
nator for go ahead.

And the message crackled on the airwaves, loud,
clear and two-fisted. At Pearl Harbor the duty comm
officer broke it immediately, and hurried to Vice-
Admiral Charles Lockwood's quarters. There, Com-
SubPac [Lockwood] instantly drafted a reply which
was coded and transmitted.

It read: *"Hang in there, Joe! We're all pulling for you—your picture is on the piano!"*

This message was received only a few moments later, when Enright was ready to order the forward torpedo room to standby to open outer torpedo doors.

Everything was falling neatly in place: TDC was grinding in proper solutions with every Japanese course change; the forward room had six electric fish checked and ready; the range was closing steadily. Everything was right until the shrill cry from the radar operator sounded in the dimly lit control room:

"Captain, target has speeded up and has changed base course!"

Joe Enright's heart stood still. He raced to the 'scope and glared at it for long moments, praying fervently that the next zigzag wouldn't open the range further—but it did, and soon.

Such were the palpitating events leading to the meeting of *Archerfish* and Japanese aircraft carrier *Shinano*, the biggest flattop built by the Empire in World War II, and her four destroyer consorts.

The incredible story of this meeting at sea really had its beginnings immediately after the decisive Battle of Midway in June 1942, where Japan lost the cream of her naval aviation and the aircraft carriers, *Hiryu*, *Soryu*, *Kaga* and *Akagi*. In dire shortage of operational equipment, the Imperial Japanese Navy arrived at a drastic decision: to abandon work being done on the new super-battleship *Shinano*, and promptly convert her to a flattop. She was to have been of the *Yamato* and *Mushashi* class, only more so, since she was the last of her class and without doubt would have been the best so far as refinements of war were concerned.

But the exigencies of war governed the building of Japan's warships. So it was that *Shinano's* twenty inches of armor plating, her tremendous 18-inch guns, barbettes, etc. were removed and a flight deck

four inches thick substituted—by far the biggest
and most commodious of any flight deck in either
Navy. The year soon became 1944, and with it
Japan's War Ministry learned of American plans to
increase the bombings in the Tokyo area. And the
Ministry, logically, began to worry.

What, the Ministry wondered, would happen if the
United States Forces discovered the giant carrier in
the area—even the existence of a giant carrier was
enough to stir up a hornet's nest. And what if the
carrier should be hit even before it got to the sea—
what then? Logical thoughts and concerns therefore
were behind the sudden rush of Japanese activity to
finish *Shinano*, at least as far as her ability to sail
was concerned, and then take her around to the
Inland Sea, the protected body of water formed by
Kush, Honshu and Shikoku. Here was an ideal operating base where *Shinano* could be completed in
relative safety—where no American submarine has
yet penetrated.

This, then, was the plan. By every law of warfare,
it was a good one. But inherent in it were some
grievous flaws. For *Shinano*, regardless of sailing
orders, was not ready to go to sea. She was a hull,
a superb and untried hull. Her two thousand work-
men were not a crew. They had never operated together. Her watertight doors weren't watertight, nor
had they even been tested. Her packing glands and
electric connections were literally in pieces. Internally, she was little more than a hull with another hard
six months of labor ahead before her first shake-
down. Her firemains didn't even work, nor did the
linking connections for her miles of fire hose.

But Fate dealt her an emergency hand, and *Shinano* went to sea.

By the same token, Fate also dealt the 1,500 ton
Archerfish a hand—and a better one. Her career, to
date, was hardly spectacular. She came to the war
zone in an era when submariners considered all the

"easy pickings" gone: when the Sam Dealeys and the Dick O'Kanes [*Harder* and *Tang*] were already heroes and when there was slim chance of a submarine making any kind of a sinking score—even a merchant score, although some few did enjoy this rare kind of luck now and then.

There were many essential differences between the Goliath and the David, but perhaps the greatest was the fact that the David [only about one-fortieth the size of the giant] was an entity—trained, dedicated, a perfect killing machine with all its component parts in smooth working order. The Goliath was none of these—not even remotely—and it showed up in dire manifestation in the early morning of November 29, 1944.

On the bridge of the submarine, Enright suddenly heard a jubilant yelp from the control room: *Targets have shifted course back to original base course! Speed in excess of twenty knots, Captain!"*

And the longshot skipper exhaled a tremendous sigh of relief as he instantly realized his fish would indeed get a workout.

"Radar, give me ranges every minute now, please," the Californian snarled.

"Range 12,000, Captain."

"Plotting Party, how does it look down there?"

"Just great, Captain!" Bobczynski enthused. "We're getting a beautiful setup for you. Everything's clicking—"

Enright swiveled around to the periscope shears. "Up there—watch for escorts. You never know how quickly this good setup can change for the worst."

Then he stalked aft on the cigarette deck, standing alone beside the 20-mm Oerlikon in the few seconds remaining to him before the dice were thrown. In his heart was the same, unyielding prayer—not only for a clean kill but for the getaway. Then he went below and took a long, hard look at the radar 'scope with the bright yellow pips ever closing.

Turning to Andrew he nodded: "It's time to pull the plug—let's go."

It was 3 A.M., nearly five and a half hours since the incredible hunt had begun. *Archerfish* had succeeded in running end-around the convoy and her position was dead ahead of it, on a base course which would put the aircraft carrier within shooting range as the range diminished.

The raucous "Ah-oogah! A-oogah" of the diving alarm was the instant signal to clear the bridge; the signal for the five lookouts, the Quartermaster, the J-1 talker and the OOD to tumble down the skinny ladder into the tower and seal the hatch. Then from below came the spate of orders and countercommands:

"Shut the induction!"

"Green Board!" [the phraseology for all compartments secured].

"Bleed air into the boat! Eight degrees down bubble! Easy on the bow planes. Take her down to fifty-five feet and level off!"

"Tell the forward room to open the outer doors!"

A heavy thump rumbled through the boat as the doors sprang open, exposing fish to the sea. Then:

"Outer doors are open, Captain!"

"Stand by forward."

Now the rapport between commanding officer and plotting party became hair-tuned. On the TDC, Lieutenant Dave Bunting ground in key information fed to him by the man at the periscope and those beside him at the chart table. All voices were hushed and fed from the initial reports from the tower where tall, grim-faced Joe Enright grasped the handles of the periscope as it whined up from its well. Slowly, confidently, he rotated the periscope until he found the dark blur which was framed against the horizon.

"I've got one on the outer screen," he growled softly. "I can't see the big one yet. Down periscope."

"Captain, range to target eight five double oh yards, sir!"

"Very well."

In all compartments sailors waited for *the* announcement from the tower; target in sight finally. But that word didn't come down yet. It still lacked an hour until dawn, and in the tricky night light it was possible for the enemy to move right into close-up periscope view without previously having given indication of being in the area. So it went from one frustration to the next, as the range steadily closed and periscope observations disclosed nothing.

At Pearl Harbor, Vice Admiral Charles Lockwood was gathered with his staff, plotting conceivable moves by *Archerfish* against the skimpy information at his disposal since the second contact report. If Joe Enright's longshot chase didn't pay off, he thought, what boats were there available in that area? Could they be moved in sufficient time? Every few minutes Lockwood would chase his staff communicator back to the radio room to see if anything new was in from Enright. But always the answer came back negative.

In the dimly lit conning tower, the commanding officer of the submarine crouched again over the shoulders of his battle station radarman. How much longer would it go on?

"Range, five five double oh, Captain!" the kid grunted. "That bastard ought to be big as life up there now."

And Enright returned to the periscope for more observations, more turning and slowly twisting about and muttering darkly to himself. But then came the moment when his periscope stopped revolving and his words were stated simply and somewhat anti-climactically:

"I see the target."

In all compartments of the submarine came the

words, *"The Old Man has the target in sight! We have the target in sight!"*

Spontaneous, prideful, these simple words echoed throughout the length and breadth of *Archerfish*, and Joe Enright knew they were being spoken but his mind was too busy to pat his back. It was whirling around the sighting figures, bearings, target angles and variance. He was sweating fiercely as he clung to the periscope, muttering every few seconds, *"Another observation!"* Then, a moment later, *"Take her down again! Bearing check!"* While down below the new figures were ground into the TDC machine.

This moment was the *raison d'etre* for the fleet-type eight million dollar fighting machine, the moment when man and machine were inextricably welded together in a common cause: the destruction of the Japanese Empire.

This was Joe Enright's moment, and it was not to be denied him although he suddenly realized that he was already too close for a proper torpedo angle.

"Left full rudder!" he snarled abruptly, and throughout the submarine a frown crossed eighty-one faces. Then: "Course zero nine zero."

To the conning tower this meant either the escorts had seen *Archerfish*, or that something was wrong with the solution. But there was no great urgency in the skipper's voice, which meant the set-up. A moment later, he steadied her up on new course and called below to Bobczynski.

"How much time?"

"He'll be here in two minutes, Captain."

Then the periscope hopped out of the wall for the umpteenth time and Enright's voice was flat, tonal —almost a whisper:

"He's a big sonuvabitch! He's zigzagging away to his own left angle on the bow starboard 30—"

Down below in control, Lieutenant Dave Bunting ground in the new figures into TDC. Then from the tower again:

"Bearing—mark!"

"Three four eight, Captain!"

"Range—mark!"

"Two—oh double-oh!"

"Down periscope—escorts passing overhead!"

But a moment later the periscope was back up again, a glassy peepsight on a black, moderately calm sea. And this was it, all of it—the big roll for the jackpot. Joe Enright sucked in his breath and felt the hot sweat gathering in the folds of his neck. He didn't move. His words came out low, monosyllabic:

"Shooting observation," he said tersely. "Stand by to fire."

Out came the glassy eye again. Then Enright squinted.

"Looks perfect. Bearing—mark! Set!" There was a moment's pause and skipper blinked the hot sweat from his eyes. "Okay," he grimaced. *"Fire one! Fire two! Fire three! Fire four! Fire five! Fire six!"*

Enright instantly called for right full rudder, all ahead and down to 150 feet at silent running. But this order was scarcely out of his mouth when, eight seconds later, the sound vibrated against *Archerfish's* steel hull:

Wrrangg!   Wrrangg!
Wrrangg!   Wrrangg!
Wrrangg!   Wrrangg!

There were no more. But those six were enough. They were sensational sounds because *Shinano* was not yet an entity. Curiously, the enemy only dropped fourteen depth charges and took off at high speed, satisfied to have driven off an American submarine and perhaps report to Tokyo Rose that they had demolished it. But it was the enemy who was *in extremis* tonight. Under ordinary circumstances, a carrier of *Shinano's* stature was capable of absorbing a dozen more pickles and still making twenty knots. Not this time, though. For as soon as the last depth charge had died away, Enright heard the miraculous

sounds of breaking-up noises echoing through the
hull ... hissing of steam, grinding of tortured steel
... and thrashing of monster propellers slowly lifting
up out of the sea.

Enright did not see the actual finish of *Shinano*,
Japan's largest aircraft carrier. He was down deep,
running silent with his soundmen continually reporting the hideous noises. They endured for a long, long
time.

What actually happened to the carrier? The sea
rushed into the ruptured compartments, and although
watertight doors were closed, the doors *weren't*
watertight. Then internal fires broke out and spread
from compartment to compartment, causing an explosion in the paint locker. But the watermains
weren't connected and the hoses were useless. Then
speed fell off and more and more explosions gutted
the warship until it was a flaming pyre, and the
remnants of two thousand passengers were diving
into the waters from which frantic destroyers
charged in to rescue them.

And so it went until, finally, the Emperor's picture was removed and the warship lay drifting help-
lessly with the wind and tide. And more explosions
and still more. And four hours later, just before 11
A.M. on a clear sunny day, *Shinano* rolled over on
her starboard beam and collapsed. She hung by the
bow for long, seemingly endless moments and then
slowly, hissing steam and still exploding, slid nose
down impotently thrashing in air as she came to
an end.

One of the greatest sea hunts in history was over.

Enright received the Navy Cross for his kill—a
carrier which had been in actual existence less than
twenty hours.

THE END

don't stop reading

If you have read as far as this,
you'll realise why Five Star
Paperbacks are among the
best. And there's plenty
more to choose from.

A complete list of titles
in this series for your
enjoyment

Westerns

 A FIVE STAR PAPERBACK

A complete list of titles
in this series for your
enjoyment

Thrillers

Occult Thrillers

 A FIVE STAR PAPERBACK

A complete list of titles
in this series for your
enjoyment

Romances

LAMENT FOR JULIE
R. Colby

BEAUTIFUL BUT BAD
R. Colby

KIM
R. Colby

ANDREA HOLLAND
B. Frame

A TIME FOR STRENGTH
N. M. Dean

THIS GIRL
J. Hytes

THAT FRENCH GIRL
Joseph Hilton

Gothic Romances

THE HOUSE ON SKYHIGH ROAD
I. S. Way

TERROR AT DEEPCLIFFE
D. Nile

THE DEADLY ROSE
K. Rich

MISTRESS OF THE SHADOWS
R. McLeod

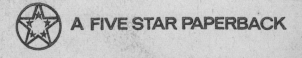 **A FIVE STAR PAPERBACK**